Brian

Haydon

Plays

Brian Haydon Plays

ISBN **978-0-909497-63-7**

Copyright © Brian Haydon 2021

brian@haydons.com

 A catalogue record for this book is available from the National Library of Australia

brianhaydonliterature.com

About the Author

Brian Haydon has written short plays for radio since 2008, and for the stage since 2012. During this time he has won awards at Crash Test Drama events at Bundanoon and Sydney, and his plays have been staged at Sydney Short & Sweet and Wagga Wagga Ten x Ten festivals and broadcast on Highland FM107.1 in the Southern Highlands.

He serves on the committee of the Highlands Theatre Company, convenes the Bowral Folk Club, plays bass in a jazz band, serves as a JP at Bowral's community desk, supervises a community Fire Unit, and produces and presents regular programs on community radio, at Highland FM 107.1.

Appreciation

When I moved to the sleepy village of Bundanoon in the beautiful Southern Highlands of New South Wales in mid 2011, I found a community that enthusiastically embraced the concept of Crash Test Drama. I had been deeply involved with the innovative form of developmental theatre for many years in Sydney, as both a writer, director, and actor. However, I was a little unsure if the concept would grow wings so far away from the city and the readily available base of writers, actors, and directors. I had little reason for concern.

Launching the first event in 2012, I was delighted with the support received, no more so than with the entry of The Appointment, a play written and directed by Brian Haydon!

I had previously met Brian through his involvement in the Small Hall Theatre community which is an excellent way of taking theatre to the smaller communities

Little did I realise that as time went on, Brian would become a mainstay of Crash Test Drama Bundanoon, writing and directing a myriad of plays on a vast range of subject matter. He has become quite the consummate playwright and blossomed in his writing in exactly the way the concept hopes for. It's what the form is all about - seeing what works, what doesn't, and how to continually work at and improve your craft. Brian became the exemplar to emulate - he can take great pride in knowing that through his commitment to Crash Test Drama Bundanoon, it remains a vibrant and active part of the Southern Highland's artistic scene.

Brian's efforts have been recognised and rewarded on many occasions. He has won the Best Play category 8 times, and he has taken out the coveted top spot in the end of year Gala Final. Beyond producing his plays at the local level, Brian has won through to the Short and Sweet Festival in Sydney – a major achievement in one of the world's largest short play festivals. I can proudly boast that Brian had enough faith in my acting ability to cast me in *The Motel* that was performed as part of Short and Sweet 2015.

I commend this anthology of plays to you – Brian's family, his friends, and the wider public. They evince the creative spirit within, a spirit I believe we all have, wherein we can tell our stories to each other in ways to entertain, inform and question our world.

But what really sticks in my mind about Brian the playwright, Brian the man, is how on that very first event in 2012, he had to contend with an actor – picked in the random way in which the Crash Test Drama process works – who was what might euphemistically be called, challenged. The guy was taking part and that was what mattered, but come the time of performance, he found he could not manage to read his lines. Brian quietly moved from the audience to kneel behind the guy, and quietly gave him his lines. I think that says it all about Brian the man, Brian the playwright, and who as a friend and co-creative it has been a joy to grow alongside.

Patrick Brennan

Bundanoon, 2021

Contents

Introduction

In 2012, Patrick Brennan introduced the concept of Crash Test Drama to the Southern Highlands by conducting a demonstration and explanation at the Soldiers' Memorial Hall at Bundanoon. The actresses in that first demonstration were Miranda Lean and Karen Granger, who were both to appear in my plays subsequently.

The notion captured my imagination, and most of the plays in this collection were written especially for Crash Test Drama at Bundanoon.

There was one predecessor – Ken Methold conducted some writing classes under the auspices of Theatre for All, which we formed to produce radio plays short videos and stage productions. "16 and 60" was written and recorded during this time, and it was never intended to be a stage presentation.

"The Weekend" was also never crash-tested. It would have been very difficult to stage without extensive rehearsal, as it depends on synchronised movements, with no dialogue.

This collection is to share with my family, sell (at cost) to my friends, and to enable me to throw out the accumulated paper scripts. The crash-tested plays are the result of pruning and editing to fit in the 10-minute format.

I had fun writing these plays and seeing most of them read (crash-tested) on stage, and nine in full costumed, memorised productions, I hope you enjoy them too.

Brian Haydon, 2021

THE MOTEL

This play was crash-tested at Bundanoon in 2015, featuring Gill Brennan and Colin Tabell in the heat, and Pat and Gill Brennan in the final. It was invited to be performed at Sydney Short & Sweet in 2016, where it gained an equal first place. Patrick Brennan played Brett, Kirsty Clancy played Alice, Valerie Warry was Cath, and Jim Cheesley played Dave.

Jim Cheesley and Valerie Warry at Short & Sweet

Kirsty Clancy and Patrick Brennan at Short & Sweet

THE MOTEL
A Ten-minute Play by Brian Haydon

Cast:

Brett – 35-50, father of young teenagers, travelling
      salesman

Alice – 30-45, Brett's lover.

Cath – 30-45, Brett's wife.
Dave – 30-45, starting an affair with Cath.

SCENE 1 – INSIDE A MOTEL ROOM

*Brett and Alice are getting dressed, adjusting their hair,
affectionate.*

Alice:	Well, big boy, that was wonderful, as usual.
Brett:	You do inspire me, Alice.
Alice:	Do you think we should try some other motels?
Brett:	Maybe. But we've never seen anyone we know here.
Alice:	I don't care where we go. This is fine by me.

*Brett walks to the window, parts the curtain and looks out.
Suddenly he closes the curtain and gasps.*

Brett:	Oh no, that's Cath's car. Oh my God, it's her number plate. She must have followed us here.
Alice:	How could she find out?
Brett:	I don't know. She knows I go to the coast clients every month.
Alice:	Is she in the car?
Brett:	I can't see . . . Oh, shit!
Alice:	I'm sorry, Brett. It was all going so nicely, too.

Brett sits down, head in hands.

Brett:	God, that means the kids will find out. They'll hate me.
Alice:	I'm really sorry, love. What now? Do you want me to leave separately?
Brett:	Who knows where she's hiding. She could be outside the door.
Alice:	Would she recognise me?
Brett:	I don't think so. You've never met, have you?
Alice:	Not knowingly.

Brett:	She'll never forgive me. She's really possessive.
Alice:	I thought you said the relationship was dead!
Brett:	It is, but her pride is at stake. She'll be really aggressive!
Alice:	Will she forgive you once the heat dies down?
Brett:	Who knows! Oh hell!
Alice:	What about us?
Brett:	What do you mean, what about us?
Alice:	Our love. We both agree this isn't just . . . lust.
Brett:	You fill me with lust . . . but I love you too.
Alice:	What does love mean to you?
Brett:	Oh come off it, Alice. This is no time for metaphysics, I'm -.
Alice:	Metaphysics? I'm talking about love. The real thing. I love you. I'd do anything to be with you. Even leave my husband.

There is an awkward silence.

Brett:	I appreciate that. But you said there was no feeling left with him.
Alice:	Are you saying you and Cath still have the spark?
Brett:	No. We're dead in the water too. It's just . . .
Alice:	The kids, right?
Brett:	Teenagers! I fear for their mental health. They'll hate me. And you, of course.
Alice:	We haven't really talked about any of that, have we?
Brett:	It's only been a few months. And we haven't really been talking much, have we?
Alice:	We are both always rushing off after . . . this.
Brett:	I wish we could have a few days away.
Alice:	I wish we could have a whole month on a deserted island.
Brett:	I wish we could go on a six-month trip round the world together.

Alice:	I wish you'd just go out and confront your wife and get kicked out. I'd come and join you.
Brett:	Would you really?
Alice:	I've told you. It's not just lust for me.
Brett:	It's not just lust for me.
Alice:	I think it is.
Brett:	<u>No</u>, damn it. Anyway, if she's out there she's likely to be very vicious.
Alice:	To me or you? I don't care. Are you scared of her?
Brett:	What if she has a gun? I wouldn't put it past her. And she'd tear your hair out.
Alice:	How long do you think she's known?
Brett:	I don't know. She couldn't have just followed me here - I went to the coast for a few sales calls first.
Alice:	Has she said anything?
Brett:	No.
Alice:	You men are so insensitive - you wouldn't even notice the subtle hints.

Brett:	Like what?
Alice:	You must know - avoiding physical contact, not letting you do anything for her, snide remarks about your getting old, parallel talk, . . .
Brett:	What do you mean, parallel talk?
Alice:	Talking about other people and their affairs, about men cheating on their wives, metaphorically speaking of course; asking what you would do if she died, that sort of stuff.

There is a pause, as he thinks.

Brett:	I think she's <u>always</u> done <u>all</u> of those, ever since we first went out.
Alice:	I have to get home, Brett. But I feel as if we're trapped in a cave with a grizzly bear at the entrance.
Brett:	Oh, shit. Well, let's go and face the grizzly.
Alice:	You won't let her tear my hair out, will you?

They boldly exit, Brett in the lead.

SCENE 2 – INSIDE ANOTHER ROOM AT THE SAME MOTEL

In another room, another couple have just arrived. They are noisy - they hug and kiss and giggle.

Dave: Alone at last! I'm as nervous as a schoolboy.

Cath: Me too. My blood pressure must be through the roof.

Dave: I should have brought some champagne

Cath: I don't need it, you know. I've waited so long. I can't believe we've finally managed some privacy.

Dave: I hope my feelings haven't shown at the office. I've been dying to get you alone.

Cath: I know. I've been pretty cool towards you at the office, but it's just built up the tension.

Cath walks to the window and looks out, taking a deep breath. Suddenly, she gasps, and closes the curtains.

Dave: What's up? You look like you've seen a ghost.

Cath: We've been followed.

Dave: Don't be silly, we're not crims on the run. Have you been watching late night spy movies?

Cath:	It's Brett. His car's out there.
Dave:	What? You said he didn't know.
Cath:	He's supposed to be visiting clients on the coast till tomorrow. Oh, hell.
Dave:	Is he in the car?
Cath:	No. Oh dear, he must have come in looking for us. He could be at the door right now.

They both look at the door. After a pause, Dave goes to the door and looks out.

Dave:	No one there. What do you think he'll do?
Cath:	I don't know. I don't think he'll wait in the foyer. He won't know our room number. But he could find out. If he does he'll be knocking on the door any minute now.

They both look at the door.

Dave:	As long as we still have our clothes on we can pretend to be having a business meeting.
Cath:	Great, ring up and order a flipchart. Oh, and invite a few people from the office round to make it look real. I don't think so.

Dave: Does Brett know me? I don't know what <u>he</u> looks like. I could slip out, and you could pretend to be . . . ah . . . Writing a report! Ah . . . ah . . . dealing with depression?

Cath: Come off it, Dave. You should be in advertising instead of Accounts, with an imagination like that. I've got kids coming home after school sports.

She looks at her watch.

Dave: This seems so furtive and rushed.

Cath: Rushed? We're stuffed, Dave. Don't you see? Brett has followed us here. He'll be lying in wait, waiting to lay into you, and drag me home to shame me in front of the kids.

Dave: I don't know. You could throw yourself at his mercy and say I insisted you come here to discuss . . . a confidential fraud issue.

Cath: You're pretty good at this, aren't you? You seem to know all about lying, deceit, deviousness. I thought you were such a nice person.

Dave: Thought? I'm the same person. Just racking my brain to find a way out for you.

Cath: Yes, I'm the one hung out to dry here. I'm glad you didn't bring that champagne.

Dave and Cath sit on the edge of the bed, both head in hands, in silence. There is a knock at the door. They both jump apart. Dave goes tentatively to the door. He opens it slightly. Cath is petrified.

Dave: (*to maid in passageway*) No thanks. (*to Cath*) Just a maid. I'd better put up the "Do not disturb" sign.

Cath: It's a bit late for that, Dave.

Cath grabs her handbag and heads for the door. Dave stops her.

Cath: Get out of the way, Dave. I'm not into this guilt stuff. It's not me.

Dave: What are you going to do?

Cath: I'm just going to brazen it out. If I run into Brett I'll look surprised, and ask him what he's doing here. I'll try to make him feel guilty for mistrusting me.

Dave: Wow, you women have it all over us mere males.

Cath: You'd better believe it, buster.

Dave: Have you done this before?

Cath slaps his face and exits. Dave winces, then shakes his head, then shrugs his shoulders and exits.

SCENE 3: INSIDE BRETT AND CATH'S HOUSE, THE NEXT DAY

Brett is reading the paper, and Cath is busy at the kitchen table.

Cath: I had to call in at the Mistletoe Motel yesterday, and I thought I saw your car there.

Brett: It probably was. I had to swap cars with George. He's trying to get sponsorship from all the local motels.

Cath: Oh! I thought . . .

Brett: Thought what?

Cath:	Oh, nothing. Silly me - my first thought was that you were having a sly dalliance.
Brett:	Ha ha, you do have an imagination. (Beat) What were you doing there, anyway?
Cath:	Oh, nothing much. (Beat) I was asking about their function rooms for Kate's birthday.
Brett:	Did you run into George? He must have been with the duty manager at the same time.
Cath:	No. (*Pause. She sits down*) Do you think he might have been up to some hanky-panky rather than being after sponsorship?
Brett:	No, I don't think so. Not in such a busy motel. Not in broad daylight.
Cath:	No, that would be silly, wouldn't it?
Brett:	Not in such a small town.

They both shake their heads vehemently.

Both: (*in unison, shaking their heads in unison*) No, no way. No way!

END

THE PRESENTATION

This play was a finalist in the Bundanoon Crash Test Drama season of 2016. In the heat, Miranda Lean played Priscilla.

In the final, the cast was Brigid Gregg as Priscilla the President, Mary D'Alton as Agnes, Juanita Manahan as Bertha and Daina Heatley as Clara.

It was also selected as one of ten plays for the Wagga Wagga Ten x 10 Festival, from 56 entries.

Brigid, Mary, Juanita and Daina at CTD Bundanoon Final

THE PRESENTATION
A Ten-Minute Play by Brian Haydon

Cast:

Priscilla, president of the District Garden Club.
Three club members seated near the back of the audience, as follows:.
Agnes (deaf); hair in curlers;
Bertha; (feels the cold);
Clara; (feels the heat).

Pres: Good afternoon, and thank you for coming along to our monthly Garden Club meeting. Please make sure you have signed the forms at the entrance and paid your fifty-five cents for afternoon tea. If you have claimed your concession rate of 40 cents and shown your pensioner card, please note that the cream biscuits are only available to those paying full price. Gentlemen, I don't believe there are any of you here today, but just in case, please note that you should allow ladies to collect their tea and coffee first, unless you are in a wheelchair. Zimmer frames do not count for this privilege.

May I remind all of you that waving round walking sticks when gesticulating is banned following the damage to Mr

Wellbilt's testicles at the last meeting. Our male membership has dropped right off since that unfortunate happening.

We are delighted to have Dr Waters as our speaker, on "The Joys of Deep Rooting".

Dr Waters has published four books, "Root therapy" . . . "Managing Moisture" . . . "Stiffening Stamens" and . . . "The Birds and the Bees – In Your garden".

I had the pleasure of picking up Dr Waters today and we toured my garden. He told me a thing or two about the birds and the bees, and he introduced me to the ins and outs of reproduction? When I let him in this afternoon he said he felt right at home. I told him we are all open, indeed WIDE open to his suggestions.

Well, enough foreplay... Prologue. . . Er. . . Introductions. Without further ado, please welcome . . .

Agnes: Excuse me, Priscilla, could you speak up please? We can't hear at the back.

Pres: Well, may I invite you to one of the front seats.

Agnes: I don't want to sit in the front row.

Pres: Why not?

Agnes: I haven't dried my hair.

Pres: Agnes, Dr Waters tells me he knows you
           from the South Coast Seed Planting
           Cooperative.

Agnes: *(to Bertha)*   What did she say?

Bertha: She says the guest knows you.

Agnes: Knows me? He tried to "know" me. Did
           he tell you I turned him down?

Pres: I think you'd better turn up your hearing
           aid, Agnes.

Agnes: What did she say?

Bertha: She said to turn up your hearing aid.

Agnes: What? The hide of her.

Bertha: Why don't you turn it up?

Agnes: I didn't bring it today.

Bertha: Why not?

Agnes: It makes me look old.

Pres: Sorry folks. Can everyone else in the
           back row hear?

B *(and others - loudly):*   YES.

Pres: OK, well let's move on.

Bertha: Before we do, it's freezing here. Can you
           turn up the heating please?

Pres: We've set the thermostat at 25 degrees.,
           and we know the hall will warm up soon.

Clara: I think it's stuffy. Can't you turn down
           the heating?

Bertha   Look, Clarabel, don't impose your
           menopause on the rest of us

Clara: How dare you. I don't tell everyone
           about your chlamydia.

Berth: You've just told everyone. You're a liar.
           You've told everyone here.

Clara: Don't call me a liar, you vicious old hag.

Bertha: Old! I'm younger than you! Your wig and
           girdle don't fool anyone.

27

Clara:	The pot calling the kettle black! One more facelift and you'll have a beard.
Pres.	Ladies, ladies, please! you're turning our meeting into a pantomime
A, B and C:	Oh no we're not!
Pres:	Oh yes you are!
A, B and C:	Oh no we're not!
Pres:	Oh yes you are!
A, B and C:	Oh no we're not!
Pres:	Look, you're behaving like the three witches.

A, B and C cackle loudly.

Pres:	Please try to play the Prince Charming.
Agnes (*mutter*):	Smart arse. She's the ugly step-mother.
Bertha:	Hey, perhaps we <u>should</u> have a pantomime each year.
Clara:	I want to be the princess.

Agnes: No, me. I could wear a yellow dress with lots of pettycoats. and lace, and four-inch stilletos.

Bertha: Your ankles would never hold up.

Agnes: I could go without my orthotics for a few shows.

Clara: A Princess with a walking stick – that's a great look.

Bertha: Where would we find a man to play the dame?

Agnes, Bertha and Clara in unison: The President!

They all cackle.

Pres: Ladies and gentlemen, we'd like to get on with the presentation. We in the committee have discussed at length the temperature settings. We decided to alternate between 20 degrees for the menopausals and 25 degrees for the bulimics. Today we have 25 degrees.

Agnes: Get on with it!

Pres   Ah, so you <u>can</u> hear me . . .
Agnes: *(to Clara)*: Her voice turns me right off . . .

Clara: *(to Agnes)*   Everything does. Turning you <u>on</u> is the problem.
(to Pres)   Priscilla, Agnes has left her hearing aid at home.

Pres: Why don't you ask her to be a good little girl and trot home and get her hearing aid.

Agnes: It's too hot.

Pres: We've already discussed that.

Agnes: I mean it's too hot <u>outside.</u>

Pres: So don't <u>trot</u> home, just walk. We'll all wait for you, of course.

Agnes: You smart Alec frump. Why don't you trundle home and get some manners and a new disposition?

Clara: Madam acting deputy chairperson, I want to raise a point of order.

Pres: We don't have points of order during a presentation, Clarabel.

Bertha: Point of order, madam acting deputy chairperson. The presentation hasn't actually started yet.

Pres:	Bertha, I have to overrule your point of order about the admissibility of a point of order.
Agnes:	What did she say?
Bertha:	She said a point of order about a point of order is inadmissible .
Agnes:	Of course it's admissible. Call for a vote!
Pres:	I won't call for a vote.
Clara:	I move a vote of no confidence in the acting deputy chairman
Bertha:	Chairperson!
Clara:	Don't be so pernickety. It's all the same.
Bertha:	She's not a man. How can she be a chair-man?
Clara:	Bertha, she's mans the gate at the garden shows doesn't she? She doesn't "person" the gate.
Bertha:	Yes, so what?
Clara:	She's the manager of the book exchange, right?

Bertha: Yes, but . . .

Clara: So there's nothing wrong with
           "chairman", like manage or woman

Bertha: You're being sexist.

Clara: If anything, I'm being genderist, not
           sexist. This has nothing to do with sex.

Alice: Thank God!

Clara: It's all so silly, this politically correct
           bunkum.

Bertha: Now now, I read yesterday that it's
           politically incorrect to use the term
           "politically correct".

Clara stands up.

Clara: I still move my motion of no confidence.

Pres: You are overruled.

Bertha: Tyranny! This would never be allowed in
           my day.

Pres: You've had your day, ... You can stand
           for president again next year.

Agnes: That would be a precedent.

Pres: Precedent isn't the feminine gender of president.

Clara: Bertha will invent a new word.

Bertha: I won't allow myself to be called "Mrs President."

Clara: How about "Ms president"? Then your marital status would be insignificant.

Agnes: Or you could be "Mx President." Then your sexuality would be insignificant.

Bertha: Oh, I don't want to create doubt about that.

Pres: Please, ladies, we are missing out on the presentation.

Bertha: Well, get on with it

Agnes: Yes, get on with it.

Clara: Yes, get on with it.

Pres: I must mention that we can't show Dr Waters' slides today. Our computer has broken down.

Clara: Oh, not again. It's always the computer or the projector.

Bertha: Or the screen, or the blinds.

Agnes: Or the PA system

Pres: We don't have a PA system.

Agnes: We should, though. Then we wouldn't need hearing aids.

Priscilla looks at her watch.

Pres: Oh dear. It's time for afternoon tea. Oh dear!

Priscilla consults her separate notes.

Pres: I'd like to take this opportunity to thank Una for boiling the urn, Carol for cleaning the cups, Shirley for bringing the sugar, Cath for the coffee, Tess for the tea, Mary for the milk, Candy for the cake and cream biscuits, Sandy for the Saos, and Chandra for the cheese.

She attempts to lead applause.

Pres: We will reconvene in half an hour and consider whether to postpone the presentation. All in favour?

All: AYE!

Agnes, Bertha and Clara rise from their seats, and rush towards the foot of the stage, where there is a cream cake on a table. All speak the following over each other.

Pres *(to side stage, shaking her head):* I'm so sorry Dr Waters.

Agnes *(to audience member,:*   Come on, let's get some of that nice cream cake.

Bertha *(to Agnes):*   Quick! They all look famished!

Clara *(to audience member,:*   I have to leave after the tea. Do you want a lift?

Agnes, Bertha and Clara shovel cream cake into their mouths and turn to the audience and freeze, with cream all over their faces.

END

Pack Up Your Troubles In Your Old Kit Bag and Smile, Smile, Smile!

WRITTEN BY
GEORGE ASAF
MUSIC BY
FELIX POWELL

PRICE 60 CENTS

CHAPPELL & Co LTD.
41 EAST 34th STREET   347 YONGE STREET
NEW YORK   TORONTO

BY SPECIAL ARRANGEMENT WITH

T. B HARMS
AND
FRANCIS, DAY & HUNTER

PACK UP YOUR TROUBLES

This play was based on the true story of brothers Felix and George Powell. Felix was the composer of "Pack Up Your Troubles", the wartime hit.

It was a finalist at Bundanoon Crash Test Drama in 2016, with Jock Bidwell as Felix Powell and Jim Cheesley as George.

It was also performed at Sydney Cash Test Drama in 2015. Here is the report:

> From Sydney CTD August 31, 2015 results
>
> Next up was *"**Pack Up Your Troubles**" written and directed by Brian Haydon. Lovely performances by Steve Allnut as George and Jay Duncan as Felix. "Pack Up Your Troubles" won Popular Vote Runner-Up.*

I used an edited version of the song, and sound effect of gunshot, played from my iphone through Bluetooth to a small speaker at the front of the stage.

PACK UP YOUR TROUBLES

A ten-minute play by Brian Haydon

Cast:

George Powell, 61, a pacifist, ex-singer and songwriter, Christian Scientist

Felix Powell, 63, George's brother, pianist, entertainer, in Dad's Army uniform

George Powell, and his brother Felix are sitting on a verandah of Felix's house in Peacehaven, near Lewes, in Sussex with cigars, whiskey. It is 1942.

George:	This is the life, Felix!
Felix:	I have to agree with you, little brother.
George:	I'm so glad we both moved our families to Peacehaven. I love this sea air.
Felix:	Me too. I just wish we had a little more money to spend. I have a wife and son to support.
George:	Hey, we can afford to eat, drink and pay the rent. What else do you need?
Felix:	I wouldn't mind a return to those heady days during the war.
George:	That was a fluke, Felix. One song. You made a packet.

Felix: Well you didn't think much of it when I first
              played it for you, out the back at the
              London Hippodrome.

*They stand, behaving as young, enthusiastic men in their
30s, back in 1915, backstage at the Hippodrome.*

Felix: Hey George, you know those lyrics you read
              me last year, the one about Packing up your
              Troubles in your old kitbag?

George: Yes, corny, huh? Smile, smile, smile.

Felix: Well I've written a melody for it.

*He mimes playing the piano, while singing it in 6/8 time.
Words supplied.*

George: What a lot of piffle! There's a war on. Who
              wants to be told "don't worry, be happy".
              That's another one for the "dud" drawer.
              Put it with the other one you wrote - was it
              "Always look on the bright Side of Life."
              (beat) People won't buy philosophical stuff.

*Back to the verandah in 1942. In the transition they slump,
aging. They sip their whisky.*

Felix: You weren't much of a judge, were you?

George: I nearly killed myself laughing when that telegram arrived just before Xmas in 1915.

They revert to their younger selves, springing up. Felix opens a telegram.

Felix: It's from Francis, Day and Hunter in New York. Mr Powell, delighted to inform you your entry has won first prize in the March section of our competition to publish morale-building songs . . .stop . . . Prize money and publishing contract to follow stop . . . congratulations.

George: March? We don't do marches. Which song?

Felix marches round him singing "Pack up your troubles . . ." George laughs uproariously. They link arms and march together, slumping in their seats and taking a drink, back in 1942, acting older personae.

Felix: You didn't mind the outcome though, did you? You got your credit for the words. When Florrie Forde, the Australian lass, recorded it. It spread like a virus. Sheet music, post cards, records . . .

George: I felt like a king with all those royalties.

Pause, sip whiskey.

Felix:	You should have come with me, touring the trenches. The guys loved it. They used to sing along.
George:	I haven't changed my mind. I was a conscientious objector when they brought in conscription in 1916. I'm still a pacifist. . . 1942, and we're back fighting the Germans again.
Felix:	Last time you toured the country in your caravan selling snake oil. No objection to that?
George:	That's how we fell out. You mocked my Christian Science without mercy.
Felix:	I'm sorry, George. but if I doubted your theories before I went to the front, I sure as hell turned against them when I saw the suffering in the trenches. Your belief of life and pain being illusory . . . that's a big leap of faith.
George:	I still believe it, but I don't promote it any more. Others have taken up the running. In America they are building reading rooms everywhere.
Felix:	I saw young men marching off to the trenches all confident and enthusiastic.
George:	Yes, singing our song. It was sickening.

Felix: That upset me, too. Seeing these chaps
            marching out to get mown down by
            machine guns.

They pause to sip their whiskeys.

George: You should never have gone to the front.

*Felix springs up. He is back to 1916 - He is in the trenches,
clutching his ears, becoming frantic.*

Felix: Aarghhh. The noise. My ear-drums are
            shattered. I'll never hear music again. Look,
            all these poor souls on stretchers, being
            carried out through the mud. Blood-soaked
            . . . missing limbs . . . mashed faces.

Felix collapses, crying.

I can't bear it. Let me go home. This is hell! Where is God?

*Felix recovers, dusts himself off, returns to the verandah in
1942 again, while George speaks.*

George: God was in pain. His creation was in turmoil. They should have prayed.

Felix: Oh they were praying alright. At the top of their voices. Praying to their mothers, to Jesus, to his mother, to God himself. Except the mustard gas victims. They wheezed and coughed in agony – no praying for them.

They pause, deep in thought.

George: How is the musical coming along, Felix?

Felix: It makes a nice break from the Estate Agency, George. Every day I'm dealing with desperate sellers and greedy buyers. There's no money around.

George: I saw your operetta, at the local theatre. It was a short run, but the audience enjoyed it, especially the songs.

Felix: My songs haven't sold for years. I keep trying.

George: It went alright in Brighton last year, didn't it?

Felix: Yes, but it's expensive. It needs a backer. Everyone was too scared to commit themselves. Battening down the hatches for the war with Mr Hitler. They were right – it's all happening again.

George: No trenches and 303s this time. There are bombers, battle-ships, submarines . . ..

Felix: *(sarcastic)* It's all an illusion though, right? An expensive illusion!

George: I'll be praying.

Felix.   How about praying for a backer? An illusionary one will do.

George: You <u>had</u> one - William Quillam. Wasn't he real?

Felix: He had the money. Unsavoury reputation. Gangsters. A bit dodgy.

George: But you accepted his offer?

Felix: He renamed the show and changed most of the script – just retained the songs. I was entitled to some royalties, of course. We started rehearsals, and we had a good cast. It was dropped when he was arrested, and he paid me nothing.

George: Why don't you just publish the songs yourself?

Felix: The songs are old-fashioned. I can't match the Americans – the Gershwins, Cole Porter, Hoagy Carmichael . . .

George: Maybe now we're fighting the Germans again everyone will want to sing "Smile, Smile, Smile" again.

Felix: I doubt it. It's so out of date.

George: We'll see.

They pause to puff their cigars and sip their whiskey.

George: I'd better be going, Felix. You look good in
               your home guard uniform.

Felix: Thanks for coming around, George.

*Felix sees George out, goes to his desk and starts writing,
vocalising.*

Felix: Dear Mabel, You have been such a strength
               to me throughout our married life. I am
               unworthy of you. You are aware of the
               money problems we have faced, and you've
               always supported my efforts with the
               property agency and my attempts to write
               a successful musical. I know you believe
               that any day now "Pack Up Your Troubles in
               an Old Kit Bag" will have a revival, and our
               troubles will be over.

Felix takes a sip of whiskey.

Felix: Unfortunately, it s worse than you think.
               No one else knows, but it is sure to come

out . . . I've been taking money from the property agency for some time now. Illegally. I am not proud of that, but I have been desperate. It seems that everything I have tried has failed. Sure, that one song gave us a good start, but now we have nothing but debts. I have to leave you for a while.

I am sorry to let you down like this, but it's time for me to pack up <u>my</u> troubles. I don't expect you to smile for a while. But perhaps you will when you remember the good times we had, and my pathetic attempts to give you a good life. Goodbye, my darling.

Felix takes another swig of whiskey, sits back contemplating. We hear a recording of a very slow version of the last 8 bars of the song.

"What's the use of worrying" (lights start fading to black)

"It never was worthwhile" (blackout during this line and for rest of song)

"So" (sound of gunshot)

"Pack up your troubles in an old kit bag and smile, smile, smile".

END

The real Felix Powell

Mandolins in moonlight
Ukuleles on the beach
Fiddles on the roof
Banjos under umbrellas
Each has a time and place

Tanka by Brian Haydon

16 AND 60

This was one of my first ten-minute plays, written for radio rather than crash test drama.

Recorded as a radio play by real mother and daughter Rachel and Eleanor Davies, and broadcast on Highland FM107.1 on the Monday Magazine program. It has never been crash-tested.

A 16-year-old – not Eleanor!

16 & 60

A ten-minute play by Brian Haydon

Cast: a sixteen-year-old girl and a 60-year-old woman, with similar accents.

The scene switches between a girl's bedroom, before and after her 16th birthday party, and a hotel room before and after her 60th birthday party

60, stage left, poses before her hotel room mirror. 16, stage right, poses before her bedroom mirror, tucks her dress up a bit shorter, then speaks to audience.

16:	I can't wait to see what Julie brings me as a birthday present. She's always on the ball. She knows me so well. Maybe that new Beatles Record – they say it may be their last! Cool! And Meg is such a good friend. She's really hip, man.

Lights dim on 16, come up on 60, stage left, who swivels in front of her mirror, and tousles her hair.

60	Damn, I'm still putting on weight. This is ridiculous. The seams of my dress are about to burst. I'll have to change to something looser.

60 goes through the motions of changing her dress. While lights change to 16

16	My Mum is such a tight arse. My pocket money is less than any of the other girls. I have to wear the same old jeans week after week, and pretend I like scungy shoes. And

all the other girls are allowed out later than me. I'm the town square, man!

Here it is my birthday, and I'll be the only one without my hair done. I have to do it myself, and it looks awful. Julie always has a perm, and Meg has a different colour every month. Hicksville, man.

16 flops onto her chair. Lights switch to 60, who is posing in front of her mirror.

60   Damn again. Now I'll have to change my shoes . . and the necklace. I just don't have the wardrobe to look decent these days.

She bursts into tears, plonks herself down on a chair. Lights switch to 16, who rises from her chair.

16   For God's sake! I'm 16, not 12. I'm in the prime of my life. I should be going out with boys with sports cars, and staying out late, and staying over at a friend's. Mum will probably kick everyone out at midnight . . . because <u>she</u>'s tired. Shee-it!

My birthday should be an adults-free zone, a free house, where everyone can bring their friends, and as much booze and weed as they can. With a bit of luck some good looking boys from the North Shore would turn up.

So here I am. Party at home. Mum minding the bar. Uncle Ken patrolling for drugs – as if he'd know. And Mum's butcher acting as bouncer. What a bummer. At least Joey is bringing his guitar – he does Jimi Hendricks. We'll have those adults plugging their ears and gulping aspros when Joey turns his amp up. That'll be neat, man!

16 sits and files her nails. Lights switch to 60. She is wiping her eyes.

60   I tried. I really did. I had it all at one stage. Money, a nice house, BMW, stylish furniture, a walk-in wardrobe full of lovely clothes for every season. The sparkling jewellery that had all the other women green with envy. I thought nothing of buying a complete outfit for every occasion.

And here I am, my 60th birthday, a landmark occasion, and I have practically nothing to wear.

Lights switch to 16.

16   I don't think my mother trusts me. Me! I don't do drugs . . . well nothing hard. I'm still a virgin, for God's sake. The boys all want to go further, but I draw the line, the same as Meg and Julie. Although I don't think Julie will last long – give her a bit of privacy and a decent-looking guy and she'll be away. Then Meg and I will have to follow, if we're to stay friends. I think Barry might talk his way into her pants. She believes some of his bullshit. He's a good

kisser though, we <u>all</u> agree. Like way out, man!

Lights switch to 60.

60   Thank goodness I knocked back Barry. Mr
            Personality, but full of bullshit. He became a
            union official, and got into corruption and
            bullying. He was in the paper last year,
            charged with spending union funds in high-
            class brothels. There was nothing high class
            about Barry; he was a bogan. I would have
            been a pauper.

Lights switch to 16.

16   I know my prince will come. Mum says so
            too. She married young and it didn't last, so
            she wants me to hold out for someone
            worthy. It won't be tonight, that's for sure.

16 sits and files her nails. Lights switch to 60.

60   Meg and Julie found some boys with sports
            cars, but they spent all their money on the
            cars and couldn't afford a decent date.
            They'd go to the RSL for a cheap meal, and
            have to watch the football.

16 returns, agitated. Lights switch to 16.

16   Can you believe it? Mum has made a non-
            alcoholic punch, in a big bowl. Full of fruit
            and spices. She's put up balloons and
            streamers, and strings of coloured lights.

Lights! Can you imagine? All we want to do is dance a bit, get legless and snog the boys – in private – in the dark!

16 shakes her head, flounces out. Lights switch to 60.

60   I'm lucky, having good friends like Julie and Meg. We're all divorced, and we get a little bitter at times. We get together in the same hotel every year. Sometimes we smoke a joint, and giggle a lot. Other times we empty a few bottles, and that's when we tend to get a bit depressed and angry . . . that's when we cry . . . It's pretty pathetic really.

Pause – 60 works on her appearance again. Then, conspiratorially,

60   But tonight we have a great idea to celebrate my 60th. A three-way blind date . . . We each bring along a male for the pool. No gays, no ex-lovers, no marrieds, no creeps.

      I've invited my cousin from Campbelltown. He's a widower, but he's steady, pretty fit, a handyman. He might appeal to one of the others. Let's face it, beggars can't be choosers. I can't wait to see who Julie and Meg bring along for me.

60 rolls her eyes and exits briefly. Lights switch to 16, who enters.

16   Well, the party's over. Mum kicked
            everyone out at 1am . . . but I got to snog
            Joey. He's older than us – he's 19. He left
            school three years ago, and already has his
            own flat and a ute. I don't know what he
            does for a living. He says he's into trading. I
            don't think Mum will like me going out with
            him . . . but I will.

16 sits, 60 enters. Lights switch to 60.

60   Well, so much for blind dates. Maybe
            internet dating isn't so bad after all. My
            cousin was fine – polite, well-dressed. But
            Meg and Julie were not impressed. And
            what did they bring along for me? An estate
            agent who arrived drunk, and an
            accountant wearing a cardigan – a
            teetotaller. It was an early night. I came
            back here to my hotel room and drank half
            a bottle of vodka.

60 sits. Lights switch to 16. 16 springs up, excited.

16   Joey is so cool. He calls me every day, and
            gives me so many presents I'm
            embarrassed to show them off to my
            girlfriends. Cool!

Lights switch to 60.

60   I got to thinking about my life. Joey and I
            started going out when I was 16. He talked
            me into running away when I turned 18.
            Mum had other problems so she took it

well . . . and she loved the presents Joey gave her. He was a smooth talker, and gave us <u>both</u> expensive presents.

Lights switch to 16.

16 Joey knocked back a gig at a pub. He says he's too busy at work..

Lights switch to 60

60 Joey was selling drugs. He built up a big business, and managed to keep just ahead of the law. By the time I was 21 we had a big house in Vaucluse. Oh, the parties we had! The older men fawned all over me,, but I was always true to Joey, and showed it. He loved it.

Lights switch to 16

16 Joey gave me a pill at a party. It was wild, but it scared me, man.

Lights switch to 60

60 Unfortunately, Joey started sampling the merchandise, and he suddenly turned from Joey Cool into a monster. He beat me up. He accused me of flirting with his friends. He stopped washing and shaving. He was rude to everyone, even his old friends. He treated me like shit. He started threatening me – really nasty threats.

Lights switch to 16

16   Joey is a scream when he's high. *(giggles)*
            God, I love him!

16 skips off. Lights switch to 60

60   I couldn't take it anymore. I ran away to
            Darwin, worked as a barmaid and kept to
            myself. Meg kept in touch and told me Joey
            was looking for me . . . well for a couple of
            years anyway.

            I'm not scared now. Joey has probably
            forgotten me after running brothels in
            Sydney and Melbourne for years. Besides,
            he's in jail now . . . for tax evasion, of all
            things. I just fly to Sydney once a year for a
            weekend with Meg and Julie.

            Well, I'd better get to the airport. Home to
            my cat in Darwin. My friends there want to
            give me another 50th birthday party – with
            balloons, streamers and coloured lights.
            Probably a fruit punch. Just a few close
            friends. Not a late night . . . It sounds good
            to me.

60 picks up an imaginary suitcase and exits.

END

Po-faced protector
Of those who would be amused
A safe place awaits.

Senryu by Brian Haydon

ALIENS

First presented in 2015 at Crash Test Drama, Bundanoon, and it was a finalist. In the heat, Fran Bosley-Croft played Mander, Wendy Hill played Axel, Neil Wright was Tony Jones, and Lana read Beta.

In the final Brigid Gregg was Mander, Kirsty Clancy Axel, Mary Dalton Beta and Jim Cheesley was Tony.. The play was submitted to Short & Sweet, but not taken up.

The parallels to the TV show Q&A is now out of date, but at the time Tony Jones and the ABC's weekly session had a massive audience.

The idea arose from a chance meeting of Patrick Brennan and my wife Brigitte, where it was remarked that all my plays so far seemed to be focussed "below the belt", about sexual relations. Patrick suggested I should try something entirely different, like, say . . . aliens. So I did.

However the aliens were not entirely asexual.

I shopped for masks and headbands with large eyes popping out on springs, to give the aliens a weird look when they ceased their earthling pretences.

Bundanoon CTD Heat

ALIENS
A ten-minute play by Brian Haydon

Cast:

Axel, geeky alien engineer with faulty speech generation

Beta, a very caring alien greenie

Mander, the spacecraft commander, serious and matter-of-fact

Tony, a wheeler-dealer with a national TV Show.

Two plants in the audience, with questions to read out.

The Play

The Scene is in an imaginary spaceship. Enter 3 Aliens. Axel, in a white lab coat, sits at a console, mumbling unintelligible curses. Beta (in jeans) is being slapped by Mander (wearing ringmaster outfit). Enter Tony.

Tony:	Hi, guys. Listen up, I have an update for you.
Mander:	You have gene replenishments for us?
Beta:	You've sourced some clean food?

Axel mumbles incoherently.

Beta:	She says have you found some fuel?
Tony:	None of the above yet folks, but bear with me.
Mander:	It's been three earth weeks now, Tony.
Tony:	I know, Mander, but the authorities are in uproar, in a frenzy of indecision.
Mander:	We chose Australia because they seemed to have a sensible, caring government.
Tony:	You've got to be kidding!
Beta:	Yes, and I'm getting sick from all this disgusting food, made from animals, fish and murdered plant life.
Tony:	I know you don't like killing plants on your planet, Beta, but on our planet all our food comes from living things.
Beta:	Ugh! How disgusting. Why can't anyone make mineral soup for us?
Tony:	Our minerals don't taste nice. We're looking into . . . mining some for you.
Beta:	I don't want your cruel cuttings and digging up from the ground. There's no such thing as harmless mining. I think I'll go on a hunger strike.
Tony:	I doubt that would work, Beta. They would just knock you out and feed you intravenously.

Axel mumbles incoherently.

Beta: She says we cannot leave till we get some . . . pluto pups? No, you know, the radioactive fuel. How you say it?

Tony: Plutonium?

Axel growls incoherently.

Beta: She says you earthlings are incompetent, and Australia has plenty of plutonium.

Tony: I've tried Clive Palmer, but his price is outrageous. He wants ten million dollars in Chinese currency and to display your spaceship on his golf course.

Axel hits the roof, still incomprehensible.

Beta: She says, how do you say it? F-f-f-fornicate with Clive Palmer.

Tony: I have no intention of f-f-f-fornicating with Clive Palmer. I once knew a woman who did - she said it was like having a wardrobe fall on her . . . with the key in it.

Axel grumbles.

Beta:	She says we can't leave your planet and continue on our way without fuel. She's getting quite upset, poor Axel.
Tony:	I know that. How come she understands everything I say but can't speak English?
Mander:	I told you before. Her imbedded language processing circuit is faulty. We can't find a planet with repair facilities. At least the other galaxies didn't have this silly money concept.
Tony:	Money makes the world go round, I'm afraid. You have to have money to get all goods and services, and to pay your taxes, of course.
Mander:	Have humans on earth always had this money concept?
Tony:	Money is very convenient. It's just like a dam of water. You save it up, and use it when you need it.
Beta:	What if you can't get any water into your dam?
Tony:	Well, the government puts a few drops in your dam every fortnight to keep you going.
Mander:	Where does the government's water come from?

Tony: They take it from other people's dams, siphon some off for themselves, and drip, drip, drop some into the dry dams.

Axel mumbles

Beta: She says we aren't interested in water. We can't run our spaceship on water. We need plutonium.

Tony: Ah, but you need to have money to buy it!

Axel mumbles a long diatribe.

Tony: What's she saying?

Beta: She says . . . "Damn!"

Tony: Look, I have an idea. I'll get you on a special edition of my show, Q&A.

Mander: What do we have to do?

Tony: Mander, you give a speech. Axel and Beta, you have to look eccentric and pathetic, and cry on cue.

Beta: What should we wear?

Tony: Just what you're wearing now . . . Oh, and I want you to wear these, to look other-worldly.

Tony produces head pieces - like eyes on a spring. They put them on, and move across the stage to the Q&A setup – a row of chairs and tables. Tony imitates Tony Jones and Q&A.

Tony: Good evening, ladies and gentlemen, and welcome to a special edition of Q&A. Please welcome my guests tonight, the recently arrived Aliens, Axel, Mander and Beta.

Audience is encouraged to applaud.

Tony: Mander, I have a question for you. Where do you come from, why are you here, and where are you going?

Mander: Tony, I don't believe you have a name for our home, as you haven't discovered it yet. It's in the 5th dimension. I was born on the spaceship, so I've never been there. We called here for fuel and gene replenishment.

Tony: Beta, how come you look just like us, and speak our language?

Beta: Normally we're invisible, and we communicate by simple energy waves. We don't use words, so we don't have to be politically correct Our bodies and voices are synthetic. Our ancestors evolved long ago with the ability to copy the appearance and communications of all creatures. We can create any texture or smell too. For instance, here is the smell of the man in the back row.

They all reel away, overcome with the odour.

Tony: Oh, turn it off, Beta, that's terrible. Now Axel, you're the ship's engineer, and I'm sure many in our audience would love to hear about the technology behind your spaceship.

Axel mumbles gibberish, shrugs.

Beta: You may have noticed that Axel's language generator is faulty at present. She said that it's a simple subatomic phased quantum drive supercharged with radioactive levitational exigencies for gravitational bypass, with networked worm navigation. Nothing unusual. It runs on plutonium.

Tony: We have a tweet here from hash-tag Femininity. "Do women have equal rights on your planet?"

Mander: No . . . we have taken over. Men are mainly slaves. They are practically useless anyway.

Tony: We have a question from a member of our audience, Mr Mundane.

Plant 1: How do you deal with racial discrimination?

Mander: We don't have different races like you. Our big issue is discrimination by INTELLIGENCE. For instance, should those who are really stupid be allowed into responsible positions?

Tony: Oh, we don't care about that at all. Our politicians plumb the depths of stupidity – no discrimination here.

Tony: How do you manage breeding, on these long space trips?

Mander: Just normal artificial instemination. Otherwise we would suffer from gene deterioration. We couldn't just use a restricted gene pool. That would produce morons - like royal dynasties everywhere. We pick up cells - stem cells, from everywhere we call. We collect only the finest specimens. By the way, where can we find . . . (local celebrity).

Tony: Another question from the floor - Mrs Eifel Fearful.

Plant 2: What about euthanasia?

Beta: Youth in Asia? We understand the youth in
                 Asia are doing very well in maths and
                 languages, but suicide is a problem.

Axel mumbles gibberish – interspersed in Beta's speech
below.

Beta: I'm sorry, Axel points out that I am
                 becoming demented . . ., that I have
                 become a silly sausage . . . and it is time for
                 me to activate my replacement and give
                 myself the flick. You creepy geek!

Beta is upset. She springs up and hits Axel on the head. Axel
and Mander jump to their feet too; Mander hits Beta, who is
hitting Axel.

Tony gets a message on his headset (just puts his finger to
his ear)

Tony: Wait!

They stop fighting.

Tony: I've just been informed by our producer
                 that the Commonwealth Police are outside.
                 They are coming to arrest you as illegal
                 immigrants. They have instructions from

the Prime Minister to turn back all boats — and ships. No exceptions are allowed.

Mander: So where can we go?

Tony: Nauru, I suspect.

Beta looks up a mobile device.

Beta: Nauru, a toilet for birds, in the Pacific Ocean. No plutorium.

Mander: I need to speak to your supreme leader.

Tony: Can you prove you are refugees from some terrible threat at home?

Mander: No, we're on a scientific expedition. We just need some plutonium to continue on our way.

Tony: I've heard of them secretly paying off refugees to go back, but I don't know about Plutonium.

Mander: *(Forcefully)* Why won't you take us to your leader?

Tony: He's a very busy man. He has to deal with marriage equality, and his personal carbon footprint, and counting his money, and posing for daily photographs.

Beta: That does it! We're going on hunger strike. Your food stinks, anyway.

The three aliens stand, rip off their protruding eyes and stomp out.

Tony: Ladies and gentlemen, this ends tonight's special edition of Q&A. I'd like to thank our studio audience, and our guests. If you would like to donate some Plutonium to our poor aliens, please send your contributions to the ABC, at the address on your screen. Goodnight!

END

RETURN OF THE ALIENS

The aliens return to Earth, and discuss some social issues.

At Bundanoon Crash Test Drama n 2017, Patrick Brennan played Mal, the naïve Earthling, Mae McKibbin the young alien. Colin Tabell and Ann Popplewell played the other parts.

Belle (not Mae)

RETURN OF THE ALIENS

A Ten-Minute Play by Brian Haydon

Cast:

Mal	A well-meaning academic earthling
Ariel	Leader of the Aliens – may be male or female
Belle	A beautiful young alien
Phil	Alien philosopher/consultant/geek – may be male or female

Mal walks across the stage, taking in the view. Suddenly he bumps into an invisible wall.

Voice from behind curtain:

Ariel:	Oi, what are you doing? Nick off.
Mal:	Who said that?
Ariel	None of your business.

Mal mimes feeling along the invisible wall.

Ariel	Nick off or I'll bop you one.
Mal:	I can't see you. How can you hit me?

Mal recoils from a blow.

Alien appears from behind curtain, dressed in bikie gear.

Ariel: I warned you. Don't touch our ship.

Mal: What ship? You have an invisible ship?

Ariel: Yes, last time we came here we were treated very badly. No one could get us plutonium. That was our fuel then.

Mal: Are you aliens?

Ariel: Alien to Earth, yes. What are you doing here, Earthling?

Mal: This is a top-secret area. I come here to meditate.

Ariel: Why is it top-secret?

Mal: That's a secret.

Ariel: Is it because of the underground nuclear facility?

Mal: What? How do you know that?

Ariel: It shows up on our sensors. We use fusion drives, so we seek them out.

Mal: You'll be arrested for trespassing.

Ariel: Oh no we won't. We learnt on our previous visit how to deal with you Earthlings.

Mal: But that was hundreds of years ago. We learnt about your visit in social history, at our socialisation Institutes.

Ariel:	Socialisation Institutes? What happened to schools?
Mal:	They were torn apart by religious and ideological factions. Our ancestors realised that drug-based indoctrination produced a more stable society.
Ariel:	You mean a docile, non-challenging populace, right?
Mal:	Whatever.
Ariel:	And arts and science collapsed, right?
Mal:	Mostly. Graffiti thrives. There are hundreds of Ph.Ds. in theoretical dancing.
Ariel:	Oh dear, that's classical collapse of civilisation Type 4. Virtual reality?
Mal:	Yep.
Ariel:	Cooking as a spectator sport?
Mal:	Yep.
Ariel:	Widespread drug addiction?
Mal:	Yep.
Ariel:	Government elected on spin and celebrity worship?
Mal:	Yep.
Ariel:	Broken promises?
Mal:	Yep.
Riel:	Two or three big, well-armed gangs?

Mal:	We call them nations. Yes. . . How do you get out of Type 4 collapse?
Ariel:	Violence and intimidation. Usually a powerful tyrant with a huge gang. You call it Machiavellian.
Mal:	Oh, hell . . .

Enter sassy, attractive female alien.

Mal:	Is this an earthling you have captured? You have good taste.
Ariel:	No, we can reproduce earthlings at will. This is Doctor Feelgood, our current therapist.
Belle:	Hi, call me Belle.
Mal:	Mmmmm, let's have a drink some time.
Belle:	How about right now?

Belle wraps herself round Mal seductively. He recoils. Ariel rolls his eyes and busies himself polishing the spaceship.

Mal:	Whoa . . . Wow. Is that your standard greeting?
Belle:	Only when mutual attraction occurs.
Mal:	How do you know?

Belle:	Your dilated pupils, your flushed face, your heart rate . . . and other manifestations of attraction visibly apparent.

Mal looks down, and tries to cover his "attraction".

Mal:	And you are attracted to me?
Belle:	Oh yes! I did a complete scan of your genetic structure. A fine specimen. A little academic, low in empathy, a bit small . . .
Mal:	That's enough!

She strokes him. He reluctantly puts his arm around her, breathes in her "scent" and swoons.

Belle:	Yes, I thought you might be susceptible to WP40.
Mal:	WP40?
Belle:	Yes, Women's Pheromone type 40 on the GAS scale.
Mal:	What?
Belle:	Genetic Attraction Susceptibility scale – haven't you discovered it yet?
Mal:	We can't generate smells like you. I read about your ancestors when they visited Earth. They used chemical warfare to

	escape capture - unbearable odours produced at will.
Belle:	Ariel, can I try out that theoretical gene extraction process?
Ariel:	We know the physical side-effects, but not the emotional dimensions. Are you confident you can cope?
Belle:	I think we have a suitable set of parameters.

She starts to undo Mal's belt. He grabs her hands, kisses her forehead.

Mal: (*looking at Ariel*)   Doesn't privacy come into this?

Ariel:	If it helps. Belle will have a scan of what turns you on.
Belle:	My scan says he likes romantic music, whatever that is, subdued lighting, low level WP40 whiff . .
Mal:	Hell, you've only just met me.
Belle:	Come on. Don't tell me you want the full dating scenario, pretending you've seduced me, plying me with alcohol and clever caring talk and gradually ramped up foreplay?
Mal:	Well, that's what 'm used to.

Belle:	Look, you don't have to prove anything. You don't have to follow those local culture rituals. I know all about your preferences from my scan . . . . You can change your preferences if you like.
Mal:	It sounds like a software program.
Belle:	Oh no, it's all about hardware!. You can't deny your basic instincts.
Mal:	What basic instincts?
Belle:	You like your females with 25% initiative, 70% assertiveness quotient, 60% vocal feedback during intercourse, conventional positions and...

She consults her hand-held device.

	Oh, you wicked boy!
Mal:	This is all rather hard . . .
Belle:	That's the name of the game.

She drags him into the spaceship, out of sight.

Ariel:	Phil, come here a minute!

Enter Phil, an alien geek.

Phil:	How's it working Ariel?
Ariel:	So far so good. These earthlings haven't evolved much since our ancestors' last visit.
Phil:	Are you still suffering from your delusions of adequacy?
Ariel:	They aren't delusions!
Phil:	Those genes our ancestors collected from (local celebrity) eons ago affected all his (/her) progeny for generations.
Ariel:	Yes, and I keep getting this urge to . . . (current issue).
Phil:	My advice as ship's philosopher is to feign modesty, and continue making obvious mistakes.
Ariel:	You mean like . . . . . (Another politician)
Phil:	Yep, (he/she) is very good at pretending to be stupid.
Ariel:	Look, it appears the Earthlings have run down their energy sources.
Phil:	There are still a few nuclear fusion reactors. Not enough for our needs. A few puny windmills and solar panels, scattered hydro-electric stations, some disabled coal generators. We need some serious energy.
Ariel.	Any ideas where we can suck up some serious energy?
Phil:	Wars.

Ariel:	What?
Phil:	Most of their energy is imbedded in weapons.
Ariel:	Oh no, not again. They did that in . . .
Phil:	Yes, huge stockpiles of explosives.
Ariel:	So they still haven't learned.
Phil:	They are pretty thick, these Earthlings.
Ariel:	So we have to start a war to harness the energy, is that right?
Phil:	At least starting a war is easy. The Americans are still trigger-happy, and love to "nuke" their enemies. The Chinese are terribly racist, the Arabs are suicidal and the Africans are threatening Ebola derivatives if they don't get more international aid.
Ariel:	What about the Australians?
Phil:	(*pause*) Oh, they are all in a psychedelic daze, re-living past sports glories of ancient times.

Enter dishevelled Mal and Belle, holding hands and swooning.

Belle:	I want to stay here.
Mal:	Either that, or you take me with you.
Ariel:	But you can't even de-materialise.

Mal: I feel pretty dematerialised now.

Belle: Let's do it again, Mal.

She tries to drag him back.

Mal: I need a little recovery time, Belle.

Ariel: Belle, I command you to clean yourself up
            and de-materialise.

Belle: But I love him!

Ariel: Get back in the Space Ship and do as I say!

Mal: Now see here! You can't block love, just
            because we are different. That's
            discrimination. Whatever happened to
            equality?

Ariel draws his sci-fi gun, and buzzes Mal, who falls dead.

Belle beats a hasty retreat into the spaceship.

Ariel: Philosopher, start that war, suck up the
            energy, and let's get out of here.

Phil: Yes, sir!

They exit.

END

Returning Aliens at rehearsal with the Writer/Director

THE APPOINTMENT

My first play written for Crash Test Drama, in 2012. It was not an award winner. Miranda Lean played Clare.

THE APPOINTMENT

By Brian Haydon

Cast:

Andrew, a man in his 20s or 30s
Barbara, a woman in her 20s or 30s
Clare, a woman in her 20s or 30s.

The scene is a coffee shop, at lunch time.

Andrew and Barbara arrive within seconds of each other, sit at separate tables, busy with their respective newspapers and mobile phones, ignoring each other, but occasionally each summing up the other.

Enter Clare, obviously running late for an appointment. She sits down next to Andrew.

Clare:	I'm terribly sorry. I'm usually on time. I had a shocker. Can I get you a coffee? I hear it's very good here.
Andrew:	Don't worry. Relax. I'm enjoying the water. Can I get <u>you</u> a coffee?
Clare:	No, I'll just have water too. My stomach's churning.
Andrew:	Well, thanks for making the effort. I've been looking forward to meeting you.
Clare:	Thanks for waiting. I've been looking forward, too. It's so hot out there.
Andrew:	Yes, but I hear there's a cool change coming.

Clare:	I don't mind when it's cool. You can always put on extra clothes, but the humidity gets to me. It must be in the high 30s.
Andrew:	The forecast was for 34 degrees today. I usually wear a suit to work, but today it would have been too uncomfortable. Did you drive here?
Clare:	Yes, the buses are too infrequent.
Andrew:	I bet you drive a fancy car.
Clare:	Why would you say that? I have a nice little Audi.
Andrew:	That's pretty fancy.
Clare:	It's just a car, but it's a nice colour. Not a convertible or anything.
Andrew:	I can imagine you in a convertible – turning heads everywhere you go.
Clare:	I think that was a compliment.
Andrew:	Sorry, I slipped up there. But I can imagine it.
Clare:	And I imagine you in a big 4-wheel drive, sparkling clean to go with your suit.
Andrew:	Actually it is a 4-wheel drive, but it's usually pretty grubby.
Clare:	Do you go off-road on weekends, or is it just city dust?
Andrew:	Oh, I like to get to the bush occasionally, camp out, do some canoeing.

Clare:	Do you go out of telephone range?
Andrew:	Sometimes. But I'm lost without my iPad and iPhone. I hate it when the GPS doesn't work. We men are supposed to have a better sense of direction than women, but I lose track and get disoriented.
Clare:	I get disoriented sometimes. I like to camp out too, but it's not safe for girls to camp out. It's nice to be in a group with guys.
Andrew:	Do you really rough it, or do you have a luxury caravan?
Clare:	We sales reps aren't as well-paid as you think. We have tents. But we do use blow-up mattresses.
Andrew:	Well that's pretty civilised.
Clare:	Usually someone has a gas cooker, and some of the guys have refrigerators in their 4-wheel drives. Do you?
Andrew:	Hell, no. But I can see the advantage – cold beers, milk, meat, ice.
Clare:	Who do you go with?
Andrew:	I have an old friend from Uni, but mostly I go alone.
Clare:	Never take girls?
Andrew:	I've fantasized. Most girls want comfort and glamour.
Clare:	Oh, I don't know. We get past that. Fancy restaurants and night clubs and theatre

dates are fine, but you know what? A picnic by a creek can be terribly romantic.

Andrew: And less expensive.

Clare: Yes. I don't know how some guys do it. They seem to want to make out they are rich or something; every date a glamorous occasion, at expensive restaurants, then champagne in the dearest clubs. Some rent expensive cars just for a date.

Andrew: Wow! It makes me feel mean. I suppose if I was really bowled over by someone I'd try to please her. It seems most girls like to dress up and go to fancy places. At school I was snubbed by the best-looking girls – they all had boy-friends with sports cars. They seemed to have a pecking order according to the glamour of their boy-friend's car.

Clare: We had that at school. But it was a girls' school, so we didn't have boys around to knock back because of their cars – or lack of a car. So you went to a co-ed school?

Andrew: Yes.

Clare: Did you stay friends with any of the girls from school?

Andrew: Yes, but most of them married older guys. Some married school friends. I see them at occasional reunions. It's interesting. All the guys remember incidents like getting caught smoking, and putting glue on teachers' seats. All the girls can remember is "how they felt", embarrassments, triumphs, desires. Strange creatures.

Clare: When we were younger all the girls competed with each other in terms of boyfriends, like you mentioned. But when we grew up it became our own careers, and there was an almost reverse snobbery. A stay-at-home husband or toy-boy became the pinnacles of success.

Andrew: And where do you stand in that pecking order?

Clare: You'll make me blush. I'm too busy trying to smash through the glass ceiling. I don't have a trophy male to wheel out. I don't even make the rankings.

Andrew: You could go to the top rank if you really wanted to.

Clare: I think that's another compliment. I'm the salesperson here. I'm supposed to be flattering you.

Andrew: Well, go ahead. It's been a long time since I've had a dose.

Clare: A dose of what?

Andrew: Flattery!

Clare: Oh! Well let me think now. . .

Andrew: Obviously that's quite a challenge.

Clare:	No. You're being modest. You are modest. That's a nice trait. A confident man pretending to be insecure is a good game to be in. You haven't told me anything about your job.
Andrew:	Well, you already know I'm a Buyer at Centrelink, specialising in IT. Nothing to boast about in that. I'm conscientious but not brilliant. Like to get a good deal.
Clare:	We have fantastic volume discounts, you know, and Centrelink has huge volumes.
Andrew:	What exactly do you sell?
Clare:	I suppose I haven't been very precise. Wide Area Network accelerators – proprietary software and hardware and some packaged services.
Andrew:	That's interesting. I've just started assessing what's out there.
Clare	Excellent! I can tell you all about it, if you have a few hours
Andrew	Amazing! Do you have cloud computing services?
Clare	Of course! And the fastest access in the business. How much time do you have?
Andrew	Oh, it won't be a quick decision. We do pretty thorough investigations, then formal tenders, and . .

Clare	No, I mean now. For me to tell you all about it.
Andrew	Well, it's not what I had in mind. Did you do computer science at University, then?
Clare	Oh dear, no. I did Arts, but got on this selling skills course, where the training company places you in their client companies. I don't need to know much technical stuff. We have engineers to support us, but I'm learning more and more all the time, so I don't need to call in the engineers as early as I used to. They meet the client techies and wallow in chipsets and operating systems and bits and bytes. That's beyond me.
Andrew	But you can discuss bandwidth and security and pricing.
Clare	Of course! But I like to get to know my clients and what makes them tick as human beings.
Andrew	So you majored in Psychology?
Clare	No, American Literature. Uni just taught us to think, and how to learn. I just think it's sensible to get to know people before you start getting down to the nitty gritty. You don't need to be a Psych major to use common sense.
Andrew	That's a fundamental difference between men and women. We deal with facts and

objectivity. You deal with feelings and relationships.

Clare   That's a bit of a wild assertion. Do you think we're all the same?

Andrew   No, just a strong correlation.

Clare   That's sexist. You think that women can't handle logic, can't read maps, can't overcome their emotions, and just stumble around making decisions based on emotions and intuition and personal chemistry.

Andrew   Do you really think women think in the same way as men?

Clare   We are capable of any number of approaches to situations. We can be as objective, as calculating, as black-and-white, as vicious as men when it's appropriate.

Andrew   I'll concede the viciousness. We men are trained to be gentlemen.

Clare   By your mothers! Your instinct is to dominate, to win at all costs, to blast away all competition and be the alpha male.

Andrew   There you go. There's competition <u>between males</u> to be the alpha male of the tribe. That doesn't have anything to do with dominating females. You run rings around us. You get your own way <u>in</u> your own way. You play us like fishermen landing trout.

91

	You are masters, or mistresses, of psychological warfare. We might be physically stronger, but <u>you</u> get your way.
Clare	Try telling that to Arab women.
Andrew	It's true the Arab women don't get a formal education, but they teach each other how to manipulate their mere males. How many rich and powerful sheiks manage to remain single? How many deal in war and peace with their male counterparts, then meekly agree to accompany their wives to Paris to buy shoes and lingerie? We are slaves to our women.
Clare	And why do you think that is?
Andrew	Weakness.
Clare	Come on! You're ruled by lust. You'll do anything for a bit of hanky panky.
Andrew	Even be subservient?
Clare	When it suits you. Come on, admit it. How far would you go to get an attractive woman into bed?
Andrew	How much would I pay?
Clare	No, how much would you kowtow? Would you miss a football grand-final if it meant the difference between scoring and not?
Andrew	Oh, I wouldn't let that situation arise.
Clare	And you think we predators wouldn't manipulate the situation so that it did

	arise? Wouldn't a woman like to boast that her boy-friend missed the grand final to take her to Paris. Or even to Ikea?
Andrew	Ikea? No, not a hope. That would never happen.
Clare	Even if it was to test-drive a bed?
Andrew	No, no chance.

They both take a sip of water.

Andrew	It depends how much you like football.
Clare	It depends how desperate you are for sex!
Andrew	Well, we seem to have gotten down to basics pretty quickly.
Clare	I'm sorry.
Andrew	No, it's interesting. It's what makes the world go round. Listen, please excuse me. I need to go to the boys' room.

Clare smiles. Andrew disappears off stage.

Barbara	The service is pretty slow here, isn't it?
Clare	I don't mind. I'm not eating.
Barbara	Sales pitch?
Clare	That was the plan. I've never met this guy before, but you know, you have to suck up and get friendly to buy some time with them.

Barbara	You're doing a great job.
Clare	Thank you. He's a nice guy. It's easy. Are you in sales?
Barbara	Yes. Telecoms.
Clare	Did your client not turn up?
Barbara	Actually, it was a blind date. He didn't show.
Clare	Computer dating?
Barbara	No, friends. I don't even know what he looks like.
Clare	I haven't been on a date for months. It must be exciting.
Barbara	Not when he doesn't show up. Actually, for a moment I thought your client might have been him. So now I just watch the door and curse my friends. I think I'll go soon.
Clare.	That's unforgivable. Whoever he is doesn't deserve you.
Barbara	That's life. A little time to think is precious, it's nice to watch the world go by.

Andrew returns to the table and sits down.

Clare	I think we've run out of time to go through our cloud computing offerings. When would be a good time for you?
Andrew	Cloud computing?

94

Clare	Yes, we are the best in the business. I can give you a video conference, or a demonstration at your office, or you can come to our headquarters. We have a great theatrette and all the engineers on call, and we can put on a rice lunch too.
Andrew	Well, that's not quite what I had in mind.
Clare	What did you have in mind?
Andrew	Well, you know, a date. A night time date. Dinner, a good yarn, get to know each other better.
Clare	Well, that's very flattering, but business is business you know, and I try not to mix the two.
Andrew	Business? Hold on, are you . . . you know, charging for your services?
Clare	Of course we charge for our services.
Andrew	I don't mean your company. I mean you personally.
Clare	What? Are you accusing me of being a prostitute?
Andrew	We've been discussing lust, you say that business is business at our first meeting. What am I supposed to think?
Clare	Listen mister, I go the extra mile to make sales, but I don't have to put up with this. You're disgusting. I'm going to call your boss and tell him how you treat your

vendors. Sure we have to compete, but you can go find another supplier who's willing to lie back and be abused. I'm dealing with your position, not you. If you weren't buying for Centrelink, do you think I'd be wasting time drinking water with you? You're pathetic.

Clare has grabbed her coat and handbag, and she storms out of the cafe.

Andrew is confused.

Barbara is smiling.

Barbara	You must be Andrew. I feel as if I've known you all my life.
Andrew	Barbara? So who was . . . . that?
Barbara	Would you care to start again?

Andrew sizes up the situation . . . slowly.

| Barbara | Would you like a coffee? I hear it's very good here. |
| Andrew | I, . . I think I need one. |

Barbara clicks her finger and calls for a waiter.

END

SECOND TIME AROUND

Another very early play, from 2013. It didn't win any awards, but I expanded it into a poem later. I liked the idea of a romance unfolding like a fairy tale, and ending unexpectedly (but happily). Sorry I couldn't identify the actors, from Crash Test Drama Bundanoon.

SECOND TIME AROUND
A Ten-minute Fairy Tale by Brian Haydon

Zelda sits on a chair. Walter on one knee before her, having just proposed.

Zelda	Walter, I'm speechless. I never thought I would ever consider marriage again. After Vince passed away I was just devastated, and it took me a long time to adjust emotionally, let alone learning how to look after myself again. I swore I'd never marry again. Too much hurt at the end.
Walter	I know what you mean, Zelda. The end of <u>my</u> marriage wasn't a sad occasion full of grief. It was all anger and resentment. Both our marriages had happy beginnings and sad endings in their own way, but that's not a reason to not make a new start. I thought long and hard before proposing, and I think it can work.
Zelda	I'm flattered, Walter. You're a real gentleman, and I'm very tempted.
Walter	Only tempted? You could say "yes" and throw your arms around my neck. What's the problem?
Zelda	Well, we've only known each other for three weeks! Three dates and you're on your knees!
Walter	Decisiveness, you could call it.
Zelda	What?

Walter	I've made my decision quickly. There's no more to consider
Zelda	Oh dear. I don't know what to say.
Walter	Just say "Yes".
Zelda	I need to think. Marriage is to have kids, or make them legitimate. What do <u>you</u> think it's for?
Walter	Well I've been reading all the debates about gay marriages, so it's made me think a bit about it –
Zelda	You're not gay, are you?
Walter	Don't be silly. The principles are the same. I think commitment is at the core. Marriage is the ultimate commitment to stick together.
Zelda	I don't think I want to be "stuck". For goodness sake, get up off your knee.

She looks round to see if anyone is watching.

Zelda (*to audience*)   What are <u>you</u> looking at, anyway?

Walter stands up and sits down next to her.

Walter   Perhaps I chose a bad word. In any relationship there are times when you want

	to escape the stress. But marriage does involve a promise to put up with each other and be more tolerant.
Zelda	If you need a promise to stay together, why even start?
Walter	It's just one of the incentives. Something to tip the balance when you are on the verge of breaking up.
Zelda	I don't think marriage vows are taken very seriously these days. Maybe the religio nuts are afraid of ex-communication, or God's anger or not going to heaven, or something. For the rest of us, it's all about the children.
Walter	And property, sadly.
Zelda	So you think people really stay together just to avoid sharing out their money and possessions?
Walter	You know they do. There's no question that two can live together less expensively and in a bigger, better home than two living apart.
Zelda	Is that why you want to marry me? To pool our resources?
Walter	Of course not. My divorce left me pretty cleaned out, I admit. But I'm self-sufficient. I don't need your money or house. I just need _you_.

Zelda	That sounds like a line from a bad pop song. If you don't need my house and money what <u>do</u> you need? A cook? A laundry service? A secretary?
Walter	That's a bit cynical, even for you, Zelda. You know I enjoy your company, and I think you enjoy mine, too. Don't we like the same movies? We laugh at the same jokes, . .
Zelda	We both hate rhubarb and vote Labor. We both drive on the left hand side of the road. We both walk upright. Obviously we are so compatible we should get married.
Walter	Zelda, let's face it. We can intellectualise all we like about compatibility. If we were incompatible that would be the end of it. Those things are only possible negatives. But there are positives too. There's no escaping the importance of chemistry. I can't explain it, but you're a fine-looking woman, and I do get a bit of irregular heart-beat when I'm with you.
Zelda	That's a worry. Are you a candidate for a heart attack?
Walter	No, I'm in good health. Although my joints do get stiff.

Zelda turns to the audience and raises an eyebrow.

Zelda	No wonder, spending so much time on your knees. Are you saying you go weak at the knees? How romantic, Walter!
Walter	You know what I mean.
Zelda	Are you saying you're in love with me? That you are like an infatuated teenager, swamped by emotions that overwhelm your reasoning?
Walter	Look, at 48 I'm not going to go completely gaga over anyone.
Zelda	That's a shame.
Walter	I'm not a poet, so I can't express my feelings adequately in words.
Zelda	And at 46 I don't expect to bring out unbridled lust in men . . . of _any_ age.
Walter	You'd be surprised. You're in good shape. You don't look your age.
Zelda	Why thank you Walter, you are sweet. Tell me more!
Walter	You can turn heads – you know it.
Zelda	You're making me blush.
Walter	I'm sure I could make you very happy.
Zelda	We don't have to get married for you to do that.

Walter turns to the audience and raises an eyebrow.

Walter	What made you marry your first husband ?
Zelda	Oh, that was quite different. We were young. We wanted to have children and bring them up in a nice family environment. We had enough in common, we found each other attractive. There was chemistry.
Walter	Interesting you don't mention love.
Zelda	Oh, I loved him dearly. Not in that romantic notion of "being in love" – of not being able to think of anything else, of palpitations, like in the romantic novels. He was a good man, caring, fun to be with. A great father.
Walter	That's why you married him?
Zelda	I didn't say that was why we married. We just sort of went with the flow. Our friends and families swept us along to some extent. It was expected. There was no reason not to. It was rewarding.
Walter	What rewards?
Zelda	Contentment I suppose.
Walter	What about in the tough times? It can't have been all peaches and cream.
Zelda	Things were sometimes tough. No money in the early days. We argued about holidays and disciplining the children. I had an eye for a mutual friend for a while. That upset him.

Walter	So you had an affair?
Zelda	No, not really. He was gorgeous, and we flirted. Vince was working long hours, and I was pretty depressed coping with the kids. He was a sympathetic ear, a shoulder to cry on. We had our opportunities, but I felt too guilty to go on with it. Did you and your wife have affairs?
Walter	Not until the marriage started falling apart – at least as far as I know.
Zelda	How long was that?
Walter	About three weeks . . . no, I'm joking. It became unbearable when the kids were in their teens. We stopped concealing our differences in front of them. We argued and sulked and undermined each other.
Zelda	And started seeing other people!
Walter	Yes. It was respite. Being treated with respect and common courtesies became such a pleasure after the vitriol and bitterness at home. A little affection was a luxury in those circumstances.
Zelda	And beyond affection?
Walter	Nothing was happening at home by that stage, so obviously a little was more than nothing.
Zelda	Was your wife playing up too?
Walter	Playing up? What a quaint expression. Yes, I found out several times. She wasn't very

clever at concealing it, and her lovers didn't seem to be bothered to be discrete. What hurt was the quality of the guys she took up with. Real cretins, phonies, weirdos.

Zelda
What brought you together in the first place?

Walter
Art. We were both art students, and we were desperate for inspiration, for creativity. We got drunk, smoked pot, did shock-art, . .

Zelda
Shock art?

Walter
Yes. You know, creating seriously incongruous situations to shock people. We would dress up as a nun and priest and grope each other in public, or walk through the college nude. Once we borrowed a full-grown pig and walked it on a lead through Lakemba.

Zelda
Were you ever arrested?

Walter
Arrested yes. Charged, No. I would explain at great length the cultural significance of our art, and get them to call this lecturer from the college to back up the fact it was art. He was as mad as a hatter, and he'd give them a long discourse until the police just got sick of listening and released us. After a few arrests they just laughed us off and warned us against inciting violence.

Zelda
I never pictured you as a shock-artist.

Walter	Oh, I became very conservative. Had to, really. I lost my first two jobs through shock-art stunts. Then I cut my hair, gave up pot and became a bore. I think my wife lost interest in me at about that time.
Zelda	And she took up with other artists?
Walter	No, just no-hopers. She loved initiating young labourers into the wilder side.
Zelda	Were you into . . . . exotic sex too?
Walter	Not any standard ritualised games.
Zelda	Thank goodness.
Walter	Does that mean "yes"?
Zelda	No!
Walter	I like to exercise my imagination rather than following rituals. I like to be inventive rather than conforming to a recipe.
Zelda	Sounds intriguing.
Walter	Say yes then. I love you.
Zelda	You know, I could never satisfy your . . . exotic tastes and experiences.
Walter	Hey, I'm retired from the weird stuff. Now I just want to cuddle and kiss and make you happy.
Zelda	I think you'd get sick of it.
Walter	Never. So what's your answer?

Zelda   Walter, I don't think so. You're sweet, and
             I'm flattered, but No!

Walter   That's very disappointing.

Zelda *(to audience)*   Walter and I drifted apart. Our
             meetings became less frequent. I started
             reading more, and drinking spirits. I flirted
             with a few men, but continued living alone.
             I don't go out much. I just watch TV and get
             my hair done every week.

Walter *(to audience)*   I was disappointed. I brooded for
             weeks. I shunned company, left my job, and
             shut myself away. I bought a gun. I took to
             the bush for weeks at a time, hunting and
             fishing. I grew a beard and let my hair grow.
             I had short flings with loose women. I got
             high, and got back into painting.

Zelda and Walter *(in unison, to audience)*   And we
             both lived happily ever after!

END

GRUMPY BATMAN

One of my first plays for Crash Test Drama, staged in 2013. I bought some Batman masks, and had all the performers wearing them.

Mark Smith played Batman, and after going home between rehearsal and the play presentation, decided to exaggerate the coughs and splutters, so many of the words were lost. Karen Grainger played Batgirl, and Brigid Gregg Batwoman, the grown-up Catgirl..

Karen, Mark and Brigid at Bundanoon.

GRUMPY BATMAN

A Ten-Minute Play by Brian Haydon

Cast: Batman, middle aged and overweight
Batwoman, his wife, same age.
Batgirl, their daughter, a teenager

Batman is a middle-aged man, now. He is sitting back in a chair, reading a newspaper and drinking a beer. His wife, Batwoman, is vacuuming the floor of the Batcave. The Batman TV theme is playing on a stereo. All actors wear Batman masks.

BATMAN: Turn that damned racket off!
BATGIRL: *(OFF)* Oh, Dad!
BATMAN: I hate it! Hate it! Turn it off!

The music disappears.

BATWOMAN: There, there dear. She doesn't
               understand.
               (TO AUDIENCE) You may be shocked to
               see what has become of Batman. He was
               my hero, and probably yours, too.
               Remember that six-pack, and muscular
               thighs? Well now he looks more like a
               keg on a rickety table.
BATMAN: *(POINTING TO PAPER)* Disgraceful! Ever
               since Dick Grayson became mayor of
               Gotham City, he's been taking lessons

	from those PR gits. Every day a picture on the front page, wearing a safety helmet and fluorescent vest, or patting school children on the head.
BATWOMAN:	Aren't you proud of him, Batman? You taught him everything when he was your ward.
BATMAN:	I taught him useful skills – ju-jitsu, lock-breaking, telephone tapping, name-calling , . . I gave him his first utility belt – a Mark 3, with a Swiss Army knife, skeleton keys, a garrote. He was Robin, the boy wonder! Not posing all day in fancy dress, with his underpants on the <u>inside</u>, opening fetes, adopting that silly politician stance, with arms, hands and fingers outstretched, pontificating. Every politician does it now. Every picture is the same. A pox on publicists, and politicians!
BATWOMAN:	*(TO AUDIENCE)* He has a point, you know. And don't get him started on political correctness. Ever since the thought police banned the term "Caped Crusader" because it might offend Arabs, he has retreated into his shell. He couldn't be the Dark Knight anymore, because he's white, and the blacks objected. He lost track of what to call native people because they kept changing what they preferred to be called – Aboriginals, Indians, then Navajo

Nation, then indigenous people, then First Americans . . . who knows what will be next. The same with the . . . I don't know, they were negroes, then coloureds, then blacks, then African Americans. We can't say "Boy" or "darkie" or "sonny". And what do they call each other? Niggers, coons and mothers.

Enter Batgirl, grooving to the music through her headphone, chewing gum.

BATMAN: Uh, oh. Here comes the next winner of "America's got Talent" – or "The biggest Loser!"

She turns off the music and takes out the earphones.

BATGIRL: Can I take out the Batmobile tonight, Dad?

BATMAN: No, you can't. It's been de-registered. There are no air bags, the rocket exhaust and ejector seat have been declared dangerous, and the weaponry might fall into the hands of terrorists. And you can't afford to fill it up, anyway. Take the Beetle.

BATGIRL: But Dad, it's so ordinary!

BATMAN: Since when did you want to be different? You insist on wearing the same clothes as all the other girls, the same hairdo, the same language, with

	every second word "like". . . like wow, have you suddenly grown up?
BATGIRL:	Cars are like, different, Dad. I like a nice, normal guy, but he has to have a sports car – like a convertible or a hotrod. They take the piss when I drive the Beetle. And it's a horrible colour, too. All my friends have, like, red cars.
BATMAN:	Why don't you just change your lipstick and shoes to match the car, instead of the other way round.
BATGIRL:	Sure, Dad. I'll change them all to yellow. The girls already call the Beetle "The Urinator".

She stomps out, tapping heavily at her mobile phone.

BATWOMAN	(*TO AUDIENCE*) Wait till he gets to page 5!

Batman turns the page.

BATMAN:	What the . . .! Suffering sogatash! The Joker is back causing trouble. Look at that ugly face! He's disappeared! Wanted for cyber-crime (PAUSE), leaking government secrets, (PAUSE) and failing to get written consent before having it off with Swedish nymphomaniacs!
BATWOMAN:	(TO AUDIENCE) In the olden days, Batman would have seen the searchlight signal from the Police Commissioner,

114

slipped on his suit, revved up the Batmobile, and tracked down the Joker. He'd avoid all his deadly traps, have a big fist-fight, and put him in jail with a black eye. He never really adapted to computers, so he can't fight the Joker anymore.

Exit Batwoman.

BATMAN: He's taunting me! "Come and get me, Fatman" says the Joker. The Riddler is with me. Just email us for the first riddle!" Email me!

Batgirl walks in, tapping her phone.

          You boofhead boffin. You stupid, effeminate, anorak-wearing, long-haired, bearded geek.

BATGIRL: Hey, Dad, geeks are cool. If it wasn't for my boyfriend Eugene I'd never get my assignments done.

          Hey Dad, are you going to do anything about the terrorists that are causing havoc in Gotham City?

BATMAN: Batgirl, you know I can't anymore. I have to do a risk analysis on every case, get a detective's permit, pass a course on multicultural tolerance, buy public liability insurance, be checked for a

	criminal record, get a certificate that the Batmobile has no parking tickets outstanding, and get a licence for base jumping, and a health certificate. And I have to join the Police Union. You can't be a super-hero anymore.
BATGIRL:	I hear the Joker hacked into the army's files on sexual discrimination, and published them on his blog, Wicked Weeks.
BATMAN:	Blog? Wet wicket?
BATGIRL:	No, Wicked Weeks. He's threatening to publish the Catholic Church's files on child abuse. Apparently they have money to pay the ransom, whereas the army has no money. Publishing the army files is just to show that he can do it. The Church has hired Chinese hackers to fight him.
BATMAN:	Where did you get this information?
BATGIRL:	Oh, it's all online. Like on the news feeds, and Twitter.
BATMAN:	News feeds and Twitter? Are they reliable sources?
BATGIRL:	Who cares? If an A-lister celeb says it's true, it's good enough for me.
BATMAN:	A-lister celeb?
BATGIRL:	Sure. Thousands of instagram photos. Millions of followers on Twitter. Billions of Google hits.
BATMAN:	Who are these people?

BATGIRL:	They are the ones everyone knows. They are famous!
BATMAN:	Why?
BATGIRL:	For being on TV. Some are politicians, entertainers, sports stars, mining magnates, socialites, . . .
BATMAN:	Socialites?
BATGIRL:	Yes, they are famous for being famous. You know, the women who wear the latest labels, tote designer handbags and have their own reality TV shows and their own makeup lines. You know, the sort Bruce Wayne used to date when he was . . .
BATMAN:	Let's not go into that. Bruce Wayne was like a bloodhound on a scent for some of those women. When he got close he was like a puppy-dog seeking affection and a pat. Then they would turn predator, and he'd run away like a frightened hyena.
BATWOMAN:	So you left the mansion upstairs and became Batman full-time, didn't you. Then you met your match in Cat Woman.
BATMAN:	Oh yes, she was lithe, lissom and loving.
BATWOMAN:	Yes, strike three. Now she's plump, plebeian and generally unpleasant.
BATMAN:	Well, you can't expect to be trim, taught and terrific for life, can you?
BATWOMAN:	No, you can't, can you? (PAUSE) You can't be charismatic, cheeky and

	charming. Nor strong, striking and stud-like.
BATMAN:	There's still that feline streak in you, isn't there?!
BATWOMAN:	All the better to snuggle up with, my pet. Remember after you converted me from Cat Woman to Batwoman, I used to go out on the town with you. We caught the Penguin together, remember? I lured him into the open, and wrapped my supple limbs around him till you arrived with the zoo-keeper to take him away and feed him his fish. Oh dear, he had bad breath.
BATMAN:	Ah, those were the good old days. We'd double-date with Clark Kent and Lois Lane. That was before Luther lured Superman into digging trenches for the national broadband network. Poor Superman, the old cable trenches were full of kryptonite, and now he's on life support, and the whole project is stalled. Lois is still searching for Clark. He's disappeared, and there aren't any telephone booths in the street anymore. SpiderMan got tangled up in the world wide web, too.
BATWOMAN:	I can't fit into my costumes anymore.
BATMAN:	Nor can I. (PAUSE) And I can't fit in my costumes, either. (PAUSE) Where's Alfred? I need a beer.
BATWOMAN:	He's out on an assignment.

BATMAN:	Assignment?
BATWOMAN:	Yes, he does impersonations of Michael Caine, and sometimes acts as his double.
BATMAN:	How am I supposed to get a beer, then?
BATWOMAN:	You have to put on your Bruce Wayne mask and take the lift up to the mansion, and go to the fridge. I know you hate it up there.
BATGIRL:	Your old foes seem to have landed on their feet, Dad, while you've landed on your . . .
BATMAN:	OK, OK. But getting back to the Joker – how can he get away with this . . . this chopping?
BATGIRL:	Hacking!
BATMAN:	Well, hacking then!
BATGIRL:	He goes phishing.
BATMAN:	Fishing!
BATGIRL:	Yes, phishing. Not with a line and bait – p-h-i-s-h-i-n-g - getting people's bank account details and passwords – identity theft.
BATMAN:	So if you don't have computers and passwords, he can't rob you?
BATGIRL:	Well, like . . yes, but . .
BATMAN:	I knew I was right! Stupid computers! (PAUSE) Cyberspace – the great void! (YAWNS) I'm tired. The doctor says I have exhaustipation.
BATGIRL:	Exhaustipation?
BATMAN:	Yes, I'm so tired I don't give a shit!

(He slumps, asleep.)

BATGIRL:	Oh Dad, that's disgusting!
BATWOMAN:	So Batman sits at home, grumbling. He can't fight The Joker, or The Riddler, anymore. The police don't need him. They have all the electronic surveillance, firewalls and encryption and code-breaking.. He reads his old comics and watches old movies, and complains that he's married to an old bat.

(LOOKS AT BATMAN, ASLEEP)

Pretty sad, really.

SFX The Batman Theme

END

THAT SINKING FEELING

This play, won its heat at Crash Test Drama, Bundanoon, in 2013. In the final, it came second in the audience vote, and Rebecca Howarth won best actress award, and Chris Jowett swam convincingly.

They play was unsuccessfully submitted to Sydney Short & Sweet in 2014.

The play was published in Figments, the anthology of the Fellowship of Australian Writers, Southern Highlands Branch in 2017.

Anton Otto Fischer painting of sinking of the Pulaski

THAT SINKING FEELING

A 10-Minute Play by Brian Haydon

Flo and Bill are obviously swimming, across stage. Both are looking around, and Bill sees something out beyond the audience. They pause, treading water.

Bill   There's the marina. I suggest we head for that.

Flo   Are you sure that's the best place to go?

Bill   The car is there. We have to head for it.

Flo   I can't swim that far. It must be a mile.

Bill   Yes you can. We have to.

They turn towards the audience and continue swimming motions.

Flo   Wasn't there some emergency beacon on the boat? Wouldn't it be transmitting an SOS? We should stay near it.

Bill   I doubt it. The boat went down so fast, I didn't think to look for it and turn it on.

Flo   So there is no signal being sent out?

Bill   I'm afraid not.

Flo   What about our mobile phones?

Bill   Have you got yours?

Flo   You've got to be joking. You know what I was
       wearing when we sank. Nothing!

Bill   Me too. I think both phones were on the bench
       charging.

Flo   I can't believe the boat could sink so quickly,
       without us noticing.

Bill   Well, we were a bit carried away.

Flo   It was good. I wouldn't have noticed a bomb going
off.

Bill   So the earth moved?

Flo   Well the boat did.

Bill   I'm glad I grabbed these life vests.

Flo   Me too. I used to laugh at the airline demos, but
       now I appreciate them. I couldn't tread water for
       this long. Are you OK?

Bill   Sure. I don't know whether it's shock or afterglow. I
       feel wonderful.

Flo   It was like having a bucket of cold water thrown on
       us. I'm glad the water isn't too cold. But I'm still
       shivering. I think I'm still aglow too.

Bill kisses her on the forehead.

Bill   If I could touch bottom I'd suggest we continue.

Flo   Don't be silly. There'll be opportunities on dry land;
       especially when I leave Jason.

Bill	You still plan to leave?
Flo	More so than ever after all this. I've put up with three years with no excitement.
Bill	I can't guarantee that it will always be this exciting.
Flo	I don't mean the boat sinking.
Bill	Me either.
Flo	What happens when we get to the marina, wearing nothing but a life jacket? There'll be people just arriving for dinner; and what if someone recognises us?
Bill	Hmmm. I could go to the car park and get a . . . tarpaulin from the boot . . . while you hide under the jetty.
Flo	Great! No one will see us swimming in with these red lifejackets, weaving between the boat buoys, will they?! And of course you didn't lock the car, did you?
Bill	Of course I did . . . oh, the keys! In my pocket . . . in the boat.

They continue swimming (breaststroke). They are contemplating.

Flo	Is there somewhere we can get some clothes? A locker room or something?
Bill	We could break in to one of the moored boats and . . .

Flo lets out an ear-piercing scream.

Bill   What's up?

Flo   Something just touched me.

Bill   It wasn't me!

Flo screams again, and starts swimming frantically. Bill chases her.

Flo   Are there sharks here?

Bill   I don't think so.

Flo   It felt leathery. And big. Coh, it was horrible. Now I'm scared.

Bill   I don't think we'll be attacked. There's plenty of food scraps about near the marinas.

Flo   It's dusk! That's when they feed, isn't it?

Bill   Yes, but . . .

Flo screams again.

Bill   Did you touch it again?

Flo   No, Now I'm just trying to attract attention. HELP! HELP!

Bill   Your voice won't carry to the shore. Not from this from this far out.

Flo   I'm getting tired. I have to slow down.

Bill   Have a rest.

They slow down and breathe heavily, spluttering.

Bill   Besides, I read that sharks are attracted to splashing and panic.

Flo freezes. After a pause, . . .

Bill   Are you alright?

Flo   I'm not panicking. I'm not splashing.

Bill   We have to keep swimming though.

Flo   It all seemed so simple! A romantic sunset dinner on a yacht, all alone. Finally making a commitment to leave my husband; making love at last, to seal our commitment; and suddenly I'm floating miles off-shore in shark-infested waters, naked.

Flo starts to cry

Bill   Let's not spoil it now.

Flo   Spoil it? Spoil it? I'm scared shitless!

Bill   We'd better keep swimming. Stay focussed.

Bill starts swimming. And after a few seconds, Flo follows.

Bill   I don't see any fins. I think we're OK.

Flo   Didn't we see jellyfish on the way out?

Bill   Yes, but . . .

Flo *(loudly)* I hate jellyfish! I loathe jellyfish! I'm feeling nauseous at the thought!

Bill   I'll try to clear a path for you.

Flo   Oh yes, the great fish-herder, my hero, parting the waters.

They swim in silence for 10 secs.

Flo   I wasted 100 bucks on my hairdo, too.

Bill   I'll reimburse you.

Flo   Oh, great! Can you reimburse me for my reputation, for my honour?

They rest again.

Flo   I can just imagine those po-faced bitches at the church! "She was swimming naked with Bill. Not a stitch on, except for a life jacket. While poor Jason was on his fishing trip. They said their boat sank. So what were they doing a mile offshore, naked? That Bill is such a womaniser".

Bill   Womaniser? It's been a year since my divorce. Am I supposed to sit at home alone watching soap operas? Sure I've been out with a few women. That doesn't make me a womaniser.

Flo starts swimming again, then Bill follows.

Flo   So who were all these women?

Bill   It doesn't matter.

Flo   It does matter. I didn't know you were a womaniser. I only surmised that the bitches would say that.

Bill   I'm not a womaniser. There's been no one else since I fell in love with you.

Flo   So who were all these conquests before?

Bill   You wouldn't know them. And I wouldn't call them conquests.

Flo   You mean they resisted? You couldn't get them out on a boat? I probably would know them. It's a small town.

Bill   Look, I don't want to name names, nor talk about private matters.

Flo   You want me to leave my husband, move in with you, and be laughed at by all my predecessors?

Bill   There are no predecessors. I've never felt like this about anyone else.

Flo   How can I know who'll be laughing at me if you won't tell me?

Bill   I don't ask you to tell me all about every man you've been out with.

Flo   You'd love to know, though, wouldn't you? The trouble is, you men put notches in your belts and laugh together about who has scored with whom. For men it's prestige. For women it's a loss of face. "oh yes, I've been there too. The old boat date? I suppose he asked you to eave your husband, too. No, I didn't think he was worth that. But you obviously do."

Bill   Are women really that bitchy?

Flo   All women are bitches. Sue Rhodes wrote that. Some love scandal-mongering, some love the high ground of having passed on their rejects, and some suck lemons and claim to be holier than thou. But we are all bitches.

Bill   I'm sorry I asked.

Flo   So who were these women?

Bill sighs and rolls his eyes. He brushes his hair off his forehead.

Bill   It wouldn't be right to say.

Flo	Wouldn't be right? You'd have them laughing at me, and my not knowing which ones had been there first?
Bill	What do you mean, been there first? No one has been where you've been – in my heart.
Flo	That's puerile. You know what I mean. Who have you had sex with?
Bill	With whom have I had sex? It depends what you mean by sex.
Flo	You're not my grammar teacher, and you're not Bill Clinton. You're ducking and weaving.
Bill	I'm not ducking, I'm just trying to swim.
Flo	You know what? Jason is suddenly looking a better option.
Bill	You mean he's told you all about every woman he's slept with?
Flo	With whom he's slept. No. But he hasn't embarrassed me and exposed me to ridicule.
Bill	If the boat hadn't sunk we wouldn't be going on about this.
Flo	If the boat hadn't sunk I wouldn't be naked, and no one would notice me coming in from an innocent boat ride.

They both look angry now, and start swimming faster

Flo	You men are all the same.

Bill	What do you mean?
Flo	All puff and posture and weaselly, creepy, self-centred, patronizing, hypocritical, dick-centric, phoney, filthy-minded, cold, crass, . . .
Bill	I'm NOT crass, but, I do admit I'm getting cold.
Flo	I hate you! Hate you! Hate You!
Bill	Shhhh! Someone might hear you.

They swim off.

END

Notes:

SFX of seagulls and lapping waves throughout.

If possible, both wear red lifejackets and khaki shorts, bare feet.

Throughout, actors pretend to wipe water from hair, eyes etc., and occasionally splutter. They don't need to move about the stage very much, but go through the swimming motions where instructed.

We wobble, worry
Procrastinate endlessly;
Love a decision.

Brian Haydon

THE JUMP

This play, based on my first parachute jump in 1986, and some imagination, has never been performed. It was submitted to Bundanoon Crash Test Drama in 2014 and to Sydney Short & Sweet in the same year.

THE JUMP

A Ten-Minute Play by Brian Haydon

The Scene is a Parachuting Club at Shek Kong, in the New Territories of Hong Kong in the 1980s, firstly outside the clubhouse, then on-board a small Cessna aircraft.

Cast:

Steve, a seemingly confident adventurer about to make his first jump.

Jan, a nervous first-time jumper, a model

Keith, their instructor and jump-master, a confident, macho man

Sam, a bored, sleepy pilot in his 60s.

Keith, Jan and Steve are stage left. Later, when they go to the aircraft, they will be at centre stage.

Keith   Steve, check Jan's gear. All buckles, nice and tight. Are you comfortable, Jan?

Jan   Apart from this thing splitting me in two, sure. This really threatens my virginity.

The two men look at each other with surprised looks.

Jan	I mean my sky-diving virginity.
Steve	Of course! It's <u>my</u> first time, too.
Jan	You will be gentle, won't you?
Steve	Hey, Keith, How many jumps have <u>you</u> made?
Keith	Nine hundred and ninety-nine. I guess I'm no longer a virgin.
Steve	Wow! Can you remember your first time?
Keith	My first jump, you mean?
Steve	Yes, but if you want to tell us about your sex life, that's OK too.
Keith	Sure. I was scared to death. It took a few times before I got the real thrills.
Jan	Yeah, it was the same for me. The first few times were hell, then the thrills started coming.

The men exchange glances. Keith goes back to checking Jan's gear.

Steve	When the parachute opens, all your weight will be on that webbed G-string. It's the ultimate wedgie.

Jan rolls her eyes.

Keith   OK, Jan, now you check Steve. Make sure that G-string is tight. No, you don't need to test the gap inside. Pull down the chute at the back. Check the emergency handle . . . DON'T PULL IT! Now, helmets - nice and tight, but not uncomfortable.

Jan   Tell me again. Are you sure our static lines connected to the pilot's seat won't rip the seat out?

Keith   No problem Sam wouldn't be willing to fly the plane if there was any danger.

Jan   Where is Sam?

Keith   Oh, he's re-fuelling . . . or sleeping. He's done thousands of drops. Don't be put off if he's yawning. He's 64, you know.

Jan   I have to go to the toilet.

Keith   Again?

Jan   I'm nervous.

Steve   I'd better go, too.

They go through the motions of unbuckling, head offstage.

Enter Sam, yawning.

Sam	Hi, Keith
Keith	Hey, you woke up! Excited?
Sam	You have to be kidding. It's boring. It's enough to drive a man to drink.
Keith	I've been out on the turps with you, Sam. You don't hang back. Are you hung over?
Sam	Yes, but I'm OK. No Civil Aviation wowsers around doing breath-testing. (*pause, yawn*)) What's with these two?
Keith	Oh, he's your typical adrenalin junkie. Scuba course yesterday, dragon boats on the weekend. Climbs mountains. Loves telling the girls about his scary encounters. Can't wait to go free-fall. Doing this to overcome his fear of heights. Shouldn't be a problem.
Sam	And the girl? She's a bit of a stunner, even in her overalls.
Keith	Yeah. She knows it, too. Flutters her eye-lashes, acts the poor waif needing help, walks that one leg over the other model walk to accentuate her bum. Three buttons

of her overalls undone so her wonder-bra has somewhere to push her tits. Weird lipstick to match her shoes, Oozing mascara. Some of the guys go ga-ga over that.

Sam   You used to too, until your divorce.

Keith   Yes, you get a bit cynical. I go for brains now.

Sam   Yeah . . . and tolerance.

Keith   You've <u>got</u> it.

Sam   Tolerance?

Keith   No, you understand women.

Sam   No one understands women. They are the great enigma. Unpredictable, fickle. Wonderful . . . when they're young.

Jan returns, Keith introduces her to Sam, and she flutters her lashes, smooths her hair and poses provocatively.

Sam   Oh God, is that all you're going to wear under your gear?

Jan   What does it matter? In the gear I look like the Michelin Man.

She waits for the denials/compliments, but they don't come.

Jan   Look, I saw all the blow-up pictures in the
             clubhouse. All naked women in mid-air, in
             formations and free-fall positions.

*She spreads her arms and legs and throws her head back in
the free-fall position. The men roll their eyes. She starts
dressing in her jump gear.*

Jan   I wouldn't mind a naked jump. I'd want my
             photographer along, of course.

Keith   We could provide that.

Jan   No, I don't think I've told you. I'm a model.
             Well, I pose for girlie magazines. I have to
             put out publicity releases all the time, the
             more outrageous the better. This looks like
             a great opportunity.

Sam   Well you can book me for that jump.

Steve returns, starts dressing.

Jan   I've heard some people get married during
             a jump. Is that true?

Keith   Yes, but we need to go pretty high to allow
             time for the service. You can't get married
             in 30 seconds.

Jan	Speaking of which, do couples ever . . . do it . . . during freefall?
Keith	It's been done.
Sam	Have you done it, Keith?
Keith	Err . . . I was married till recently, and my wife didn't like parachuting.
Sam	So?
Jan	I bet he has. Nine hundred and ninety-nine jumps, and all that stirred up testosterone?
Keith	Time to go, folks. We have to repeat all checks. Go. Sam, all refuelled?
Sam.	Sure.

They check straps, and stride around to the far side of the imaginary Cessna and climb in. Sam is Stage left in front, Steve next to him and last to enter. Keith and Jan are behind. All are on seats except Steve, who kneels on the floor of the plane.

Steve	Hey, where's my seat?
Keith	You kneel, but you're first out, so don't worry. It's a Cessna, not a jumbo jet. Here, let me attach your static lines to Sam's seat.

Sam starts the engine, and they jiggle to show he is taxiing.

Sam   VR-HOT to tower. Request permission to take off for para drop.

Control Tower *(it can be Keith, from the back seat behind Sam, imitating radio sound)* Ten minute delay, old chap, The Chaplain hasn't finished his sermon yet.

They sit in silence. Sam yawns, Jan touches up her make-up, Steve fidgets, Keith looking at his watch every few seconds.

Control Tower   Cleared to take off. He finished early.

They imitate a take-off, leaning back in unison at lift-off. They have to yell, now, over the engine.

Steve   It's bloody windy. Can I close the door?

Sam   There is no door, mate. These are really stripped down. You have to climb out there.

Steve   Shit! It was so much easier jumping off chairs at training.

Sam   Just going through a thousand feet.

Jan   A thousand feet? How high do we go?

Keith   Just over two thousand

Jan looks out the window. Steve is looking a bit scared.

Jan   It's so far down

Steve   My mouth's gone dry. Got any water?

Sam   I'll call the stewardess . . .This isn't Cathay
                 Pacific, you know.

They continue jolting about for a while

Sam   Sorry, a bit of turbulence.

Jan   Are we parachuting through this on the way
                 down?

Keith   You won't even notice it.

*Keith puts his goggles on, clambers forward, between Jan
                 and Steve, looking out the missing door.*

Sam   Two thousand three hundred feet. Over
                 target in twenty seconds.

*Keith waits 5 seconds then throws his marker out. It has a
long ribbon attached. He peers out as it descends.*

Keith   Gee, the wind is strong. We might have to
                 abort.

Sam   What, on your 1000th jump?

Keith	Last weekend's freefall was supposed to be my 1000th, but the typhoon warning killed that. Allow for the wind, and give me ten seconds to engine cut.
Jan and Steve	Engine cut?
Keith	Normal procedure. When he cuts, you stand on your left leg on the wheel cover, grasp the wing strut just like in the training video, and when I say "jump" you jump.
Steve	Yes, sir!
Sam	Ten seconds to cut.
Keith	Here we go. Remember goggles on, head back, arms and legs back, see you in the bar.

All goes quiet, just wind noise. Steve adjusts his goggles and climbs out, facing audience, holding imaginary strut, responding to the air resistance.

Steve	Whoooah. The wind, I can't hold on.
Keith	Hang in there, Steve, it's not for long. Three, two, one, JUMP.

Steve freezes.

Steve	I can't let go!
Keith	Jump, damn it.
Steve	I can't!
Keith	Shit! Hang on tight. We'll have to go round . . . Go round, Sam.

Nothing happens

Keith	Sam, go round.

Keith looks at Sam and gasps. Sam is slumped in his seat.

Keith	Oh, shit! He's passed out.

Jan screams.

Keith	Sam, wake up! Wake up! Steve, come back in!
Steve	I can't. I can't. Is the pilot dead?

Jan screams again.

Jan	We're going to die!
Keith	Steve, you've got to jump before we get too far away. Go, man, go . . . GO!

Keith kicks Steve and he lets go, howling as he disappears off stage right.

Jan screams again.

Jan   Murderer! You kicked him out.

Keith   Can you fly this plane?

Jan   No! You bastard! You kicked him out.

Keith   You'll have to go too. Be brave. I won't kick
                you if you jump yourself.

Jan screams and splutters.

Jan   Alright, I'll go.

Jan climbs into place, quickly jumps, screaming all the way off stage right, scream dying away. Keith shakes Sam, but he doesn't respond.

Keith   Shit, Sam, I thought you might be fooling
                again.

Sam opens his eyes and sits up.

Sam   I was. Couldn't have you doing a low level
                static line for your 1000th jump. Just not
                right.

Sam and Keith lurch as the plane stalls and goes into a dive. Keith nearly falls out as Sam switches on the motor and powers out of the stall.

Keith   Damn. It's too low to jump now. Take me back up.

Sam   Don't be silly. That's no way to celebrate your 1000th jump. It's got to be a high level free fall with a good crew.

Keith   Sam, you old bastard. You faked that blackout just to stop me jumping? I was dreading having to land the plane, and I feared you'd get grounded as a medical risk.

Sam   Or worse still, I would have been breathalysed.

Keith   You'd better get on the blower and make sure those kids made it OK. I'll have to explain the psychological prompting to Civil Aviation again.

Sam pulls out a cigar and lights it.

Sam   Stop worrying. We'll have a hell of a celebration next week. No beginners, and Sandy and Jill have promised to jump naked again.

Keith   Zowee!

Sam   We've got the big military plane that we
had to cancel last week

Keith   Sold

They shake hands.

END

Moment of truth.

Static Line first jump

Hope springs eternal;
Flowers bloom in the springtime;
Lonely folk still weep.

Senryu by Brian Haydon

MOTHERS' DAY PRESENT

Read at Bundanoon Crash Test Drama in 2014, and at a meeting of the Fellowship of Australian Writers, Southern Highlands Branch. It was timely, with Mothers' Day just around the corner. I wish I could remember the cast.

MOTHERS' DAY PRESENT

A Ten-Minute Play by Brian Haydon

Cast

Fred Turnity, 32, a lawyer.
Tilly Turnity, his sister, 20-35.

Scene

A coffee shop.

Fred:	So, Sis, what's the big issue you wanted to discuss?
Tilly:	Mothers' Day, Fred. It's coming up soon.
Fred:	Shit, Tilly. I thought it was going to be something important!
Tilly:	It is important. The one day of the year we can honour Mum.
Fred:	What? What about her birthday, and Xmas? We honour her then. I honour her every day!
Tilly:	You think you honour her by just being around all the time. Whoever heard of a 32-year-old lawyer living at home with his mother?
Fred:	She loves having me around. Gives her something to complain about.
Tilly:	And you give her plenty to complain about.

152

Fred jumps to his feet.

Fred: What do you mean? I try to deprive her of excuses to complain. It's a challenge.

Tilly: Sure, you leave a mess for her to clean up, you leave the heater on all day, you traipse mud through the house on wet days, you leave your underwear for her to pick up, you never put the toilet seat down, your skidmarks . . .

Fred: Hey, you sound just _like_ Mum! Are you doing an apprenticeship with her? I can just see the apprentice syllabus: How to take offence unnecessarily; how to put on a pooey, secrets of the silent treatment; anal attention to minor detail; advanced harping . . .

Tilly gets up, wagging her finger.

Tilly: Look, someone has to stick up for her. Since Dad left, you've given her hell.

Fred: Dad didn't leave, he was kicked out.

Tilly: Whatever! It had to be. All they did was argue.

Fred: That's all _we_ do. It must be genetic.

Tilly sits down again.

Tilly: You give her hell, and she gives you all your meals, you washing, your ironing, your clothes sorting, your shopping. She even does the garden,

Fred: I mow the lawn!

Tilly: Oh yes, and you change the light globes, too, don't you?

Fred: Yes, and I fix the internet when she gets flustered.

Tilly: Yes, but only after she gets herself into a frenzy. She even cleans your shoes!

Fred: I don't <u>want</u> my shoes cleaned. It's unfashionable.

Tilly's telephone rings. She stands up and answers it.

Tilly: No I don't want to buy my mother solar heating for Mother's Day. Go to hell!

She hangs up and switches the phone off.

Fred: I've got to go out.

Tilly: How much do you give her for rent?

Fred: What? None of your business.

Tilly: It <u>is</u> my business. She's never got any money. And where does all <u>your</u> money go?

Fred sits down, sighing.

Fred: I'm saving up for a house.

Tilly: For you and Mum?

Fred: Don't be silly. For when I have a family and kids.

Tilly: God! I pity your wife! She'd have to be blind, deaf and have no sense of smell.

Fred: Well strike 3! Where does <u>your</u> money go?

Tilly: On rent, mainly. Oh, and food, electricity, haircuts, and a few nice clothes, gifts for friends, dry cleaning, cleaning materials, telephone plan . .   but you wouldn't understand any of those things, Mummy's Boy.

Fred: I pay for my telephone! And my clothes.

Tilly: Rubbish! Mum gives you socks and underpants for your birthday, and a swimming costume every Xmas, and your only suit when you graduated - because you are always so daggy.

Fred: She buys me swimming costumes because doesn't like my budgy smugglers.

Tilly: Either do I. They are disgusting!

155

Fred stands up again, on the attack. He camps it up a bit.

Fred: What about you and your boyfriends? You always go for the fashion freaks. The expensive suits, the silk ties and starched shirts, Yuk!

Tilly: I like men with a bit of pride . . .

Fred: Pride?

Tilly: Pride in their appearance, and some taste and style.

Fred: And you're <u>still</u> looking for a <u>straight</u> one!

Tilly: Yes.

Fred sits down again.

Fred: Look, don't get me wrong. I love Mum. I'd rescue her from any danger. While I'm here I can protect her.

Tilly: What from? The Day of the Triffids? Solar energy salesmen? Mormons? Potential husbands?

Fred: Yeah, sure. As if anyone would want to crack on to Mum.

Tilly: You might be surprised.

Fred springs up, enthusiastic and animated.

Fred: Maybe she could try internet dating? I can
         just imagine . . . confirmed cynic, likes
         dancing but prefers to lead, reformed
         misandrist, . . . seeks dashing, well-dressed,
         tidy, house-trained handyman, with
         conservative taste in music, well versed in
         celebrities and soap operas, who
         appreciates the finer things in life, like
         handbags, women's shoes, earrings and
         soap powders, to share nights at home in
         front of the television, and romantic dinners
         at home under a fluorescent light. Must not
         be over-sexed.

Tilly: You're cruel. And you forgot the need to
         tolerate fans and cold wraps and anything
         else to cool down Except air-conditioning,
         of course, because she can't afford it!

Fred: How do menopausal women find good
         men, anyway?

Tilly stands up.

Tilly: They don't!

Fred sits down again

Fred:	I don't think this is what you wanted to discuss. Or did you have in mind a gift card to e-Harmony, or Match.com?
Tilly:	Fred, you surprise me! How do you know about those dating sites?
Fred:	I just looked up Google.
Tilly:	Oh, yes. Google, everything you need to know - in a brown-paper bag.
Fred:	No, really. I looked up the top 10 in Australia. I found a couple for Mum. Love again.com, with a picture of an old couple, and what about "It's nice to be naughty.com"?
Tilly:	Cruel. You realise she and Dad had to have a bit of hanky-panky to conceive you, don't you?
Fred:	And you can't be a virgin birth, so that's at least two . . .
Tilly:	Presents, Fred. I want to discuss presents. It wouldn't look right if we both gave her the same present.
Fred:	Fat chance of that.
Tilly:	What did you have in mind, apart from a gift voucher to a mating site?
Fred:	Mating site? That sounds terrible.
Tilly:	You know what I mean.
Fred:	Dating.

Tilly:	Yes, but I can't imagine Mum dating, as such.
Fred:	Or mating, for that matter. I was only kidding.
Tilly:	So what else _did_ you have in mind?
Fred:	Umm umm. What did _you_ have in mind?
Tilly:	You wouldn't understand. Cute little trinkets and craftwork from the markets; her favourite soap, an aromatic candle, a new night-gown, a gossip magazine . . . thoughtful, personal things
Fred:	What a lot of crap
Tilly:	OK, come on then . . . . a bottle of champagne?
Fred _(nodding)_	Yeah
Tilly	A box of chocolates?
Fred _(nodding)_	Yeah!
Tilly	_Your_ favourite wire to _share_?
Fred _(nodding)_	Well, maybe . . .
Tilly	Flowers?
Fred _(nodding)_	She loves them!
Tilly	Lunch at the local pub? With her loving son, Noddy?
Fred:	_One_ of the above – not _all_ of them at once!
Tilly:	You are so imaginative!

Fred:	Hey, and you're good. You got them all. . . . But I <u>can</u> resist those Mothers Day sale ads for washing machines, steam cleaners, coffee makers and deluxe dustpans.
Tilly:	So no original ideas, eh?
Fred:	I saw an ad for Gorilla-grams.
Tilly:	Hmm, . . . Male Stripper-grams are all the rage now.
Fred:	Yes, I don't think Mum would want one of those. Nor would I.
Tilly:	<u>You'd</u> feel pretty inadequate if a male stripper-gram arrived.
Fred:	Oh, I don't know. He'd just strip down to his budgie smugglers, wouldn't he? Mum's seen them before, with me at home.
Tilly:	They don't stop at their underwear today, Fred. They go all the way!
Fred:	How disgusting!
Tilly:	Look, we owe Mum a decent Mother's Day this year, after last year's disaster.
Fred:	You mean when Dad turned up with roses, as if it was Valentine's Day?
Tilly:	And pressed Mum for a reconciliation.
Fred:	Perhaps that would have been the perfect Mother's Day gift.
Tilly:	You're joking.

Fred:	Mum would be happy. She'd have someone else to whinge about instead of me.
Tilly:	He'd kick you out n a jiff.
Fred:	No, he likes my company.
Tilly:	He's not coming again is he?
Fred:	No, he's promisec. In fact, he invited us both for a few days on Hamilton Island next weekend.
Tilly:	But that coincides with . . .
Fred:	Mother's Day. Yes. I was tempted, but I declined.
Tilly:	Do you think he did it on purpose?
Fred:	No, just ignorance . . ., naivety . . ., callous apathy.
Tilly:	Hmm, like father, like son.
Fred:	(*PAUSE*) Now you're being cruel. Have you thought to ask her what she'd really like?
Tilly:	I did, actually.
Fred:	And?
Tilly:	Well, you know she was adopted as a baby, and then had a none-too nice step-mother?
Fred:	Auntie Dorothy? The wicked witch of the Western Suburbs?
Tilly:	Yes, well I don't know that Mum ever called her that.
Fred:	No, it rhymed with "witch" though.

Tilly:	She wants a quiet dinner at home; and she wants to cook.
Fred:	No, we should take her out. And no Auntie Dorothy.
Tilly:	She wants to open that old bottle of Grange that's been in the cupboard for about 10 years.
Fred:	Sacrilege! Neither of you would appreciate that! Dad bought that for a special occasion!'
Tilly:	She has a special surprise for us.
Fred:	For us? It's supposed to be <u>her</u> day!
Tilly:	If it makes her happy, why not?
Fred:	What sort of surprise? Lobster thermidor? Tiramisu?
Tilly:	Not food. She just wants to surprise us.
Fred:	But you know?
Tilly:	Yes.
Fred:	So come on, then.
Tilly:	It's a secret.
Fred:	A secret! That means you've told all your girlfriends.

Tilly jumps to her feet.

Tilly:	Rubbish! . . . Only Angela and Susie, actually.

Fred:	Oh yes, the Twitter Twins. It'll have gone viral by now.
Tilly:	Oh, I'm so excited! I helped her set it up.
Fred:	Come on, Tilly, I won't tell anyone.
Tilly:	Sure.
Fred:	Give me a teeny clue.
Tilly:	She's meeting someone for the first time.
Fred:	A blind date? You set up a blind date for her on Mothers' Day? As a present?
Tilly:	Don't be so insensitive.
Fred:	Is it one of the men around here? They are pretty unimpressive.
Tilly:	No. It's a woman.
Fred:	You mean, . . . Mum's a . . .
Tilly:	Fred, you're crass.
Fred:	I don't understand. You've helped Mum set it up. A blind date with a woman.
Tilly:	(*pause*) I helped Mum trace her birth mother. (*pause*) She's coming to <u>our</u> place for Mother's Day to meet Mum, and Mum's so excited that she'll get to meet <u>us</u>, too. Can you think of a better Mother's Day present, for <u>both</u> of them?
Fred:	(*pause, agape*) Wow!

END

PRIDE & THE PREFECT

Pride and Prejudice, by Jane Austen, provided the basis for this play, as well as Suzy Bate, the salesperson who sold me my Subaru at Moss Vale. My grandmother's beloved Ford Prefect was also an inspiration.

At Sydney Crash Test Drama, Nick Subjak played the hotrod, and burst into his entrance only to go head over turkey. It brought the house down, and the laughter went on for several minutes. It was his first acting part, I think, and as the years went by he became an award-winning actor. The play was disqualified for taking too long, so I had to remove some parts. This is the final edited version, renamed to emphasise the Jane Austen metaphor. The report from Sydney read:

Aug 4, 2014 CTD SYD

*Sixth for the night was "**The Caryard**" by newcomer Brian Haydon. Tom Richards directed Julie-Anne Breen, Carli Carey and Nick Subjak in this cute script about three anthropomorphised cars.*

At Bundanoon, in the heat, Norbert Belley played Rod, Miranda Lean the prefect. The play was a finalist in 2014, with Jim Cheesley as the hotrod.

I spent many hours on the car pictures. There was a front view and a back view of each car. The colour of the Anglia was based on Bill Swingler's first car.

Miranda Lean, Norbert Belley and Rebecca Howarth at Bundanoon CTD

Julie-Anne, Carey & Nick at Sydney CTD

PRIDE & THE PREFECT

A Ten-Minute Play by Brian Haydon

Cast:

Prefect	An elderly 1959 Ford Prefect 107E. Proud, snobbish (female).
Anglia	A 1959 Ford Anglia. Cynical, been around. (female)
Rod	A black Ford Anglia Hot-rod. Hip, vain. (male)

Director's Introduction (voice over):

> It is a truth universally acknowledged, that a single man in possession of a good fortune must be in want of a car. The Scene is a used car yard. Mrs Benneton is the sales manager. She wants to see each of her cars go to a good owner, as quickly as possible . . . for a good price of course.

Enter Prefect and Anglia, parking beside each other, facing the audience. They may have price stickers on them

Anglia	What's up with you, Prefect? You look like a geriatric going on a date.
Prefect	I am, indeed, Anglia. That nice young sales assistant just gave me a polish and make-up.
Anglia	That mascara on your tyres is very sexy. Is something special happening today?

Prefect	Mrs Benneton must have a good sales prospect coming for a test drive. I'm due for some TLC. I had such a wonderful owner in old Mr Sparkle.
Both *(in unison)*	Fifty years with one owner.
Anglia	You were lucky. I had divorce after divorce. All my owners traded me in on younger models, despite my being faithful . . . most of the time.
Prefect	Well, that's men for you. Mr Sparkle used to . . .
Both *(in unison)*:	wash me every week.
Anglia	Yes, I know.
Prefect	Yes. And a ...
Both *(in unison)*	polish on the first of the month.
Anglia	Yes, I know.
Prefect	Mr Sparkle used to look after my insides, too. He'd take me to this place with giant vacuum machines advertising "more suck for your buck".

They both pucker their lips in delight.

Anglia	How are your feet? New brakes? Your shoes are looking good.
Prefect	Yes. Good old standard 155 by 13 Dunlops.
Anglia	I only had the cheapest shoes going. Chinese crap. Needed inner tubes.
Prefect	At least you had electric wipers.
Anglia	Yes, thank goodness. You had the old vacuum type that slowed down when you went up hills. I bet you still have them.
Prefect	Of course I do. I'm original.
Anglia	Another word for outdated.
Prefect	Hmmph! But we both suffered the same problems down below, didn't we?.
Anglia	Oh, don't remind me. I had chemo therapy . . . but the rust just kept spreading. It was only when the flatulence got really noisy that we'd be put in hospital, raised on stirrups, and have our tubes cut out.
Prefect	Very un-ladylike if you ask me.
Anglia	And that period of overheating we all go through.
Prefect	I'm over it now.

Anglia	Me too. Sometimes I got so hot I blew a gasket. Embarrassing.
Prefect	Me too. But I think we both look pretty good for our age. 1959 was a good year. I thought those American cars of the 50s and 60s were tacky.
Anglia	Yes, big hipped mommas.
Prefect	Topless
Anglia	Four-eyed
Prefect	High maintenance!
Anglia	Oh, they were cheap to buy in America. Even the kids had flash cars.
Prefect	Cheap, cheap, cheap. I cost 600 pounds new.
Anglia	And what are you worth now? Not much, I'm afraid.
Prefect	Someone must want a well-preserved lady in her 50s.
Anglia	There's someone for everyone. That's what Mrs Benneton says.

(OFF) The sound of a noisy exhaust revving up

Prefect	Ooh, what's that racket? Someone must have blown a muffler.

Enter a black, Ford Anglia Hot Rod. It races up to the other two cars and brakes suddenly next to Anglia. He combs his hair, Fonze style.

Rod	Hi, guys. What's cookin'?
Prefect	Oh dear, there goes the neighbourhood.
Rod	Hi. I'm Rod. At the car club they call me Hot . . . Rod.
Prefect	You're not , . . . <u>or ginal</u>, are you?
Rod	Nope. Got souped up real fine. Lowered suspension, twin carbs, double exhaust . . .
Prefect	Do you have a problem in your . . . posterior?
Rod	No, I've got studded leather interior, carpet, the works.
Anglia	She means your arse, mate. You farted all the way into the caryard.

Prefect looks disgusted at this coarse outburst.

Rod	Oh, my <u>tone</u>. The guys love my deep-throated power-packed rumble, and the girls love the throbbing sound in synch with the vibrations . . .
Prefect	That's quite enough, thank you. You are coarse . . . and loud.
Rod	Loud? You bet. I have an FM radio with four speakers. Did you guys ever get upgraded with a radio?

171

| Prefect | How degrading! That wouldn't be <u>original</u>. And all those terrible sounds, and drilling through your skin for an aerial. No thanks. |
| Anglia | I would have liked a radio, and a shiny skin like yours. |

Anglia strokes Rod's skin. Prefect winces.

Anglia	Prefect, you don't seem to like Rod.
Prefect	I don't mind him. It's just that he's . . . black.
Anglia	What's wrong with black?
Prefect	It's not even a standard Ford colour.
Anglia	Our ancestors were <u>all</u> black. You could have a Ford in any colour, as long as it was black.
Rod	Your paint looks OK. I don't dig the colour though. Turquoise and white. Yuk!
Anglia	Oh, I was lucky. I got restored by a Car Club guy. Original colour. He took me to car club rallies all over the state.
Rod	Lucky you! Hot rodders and car club guys are the perfect husbands. Do you think we'll score one here?
Anglia	Mrs Benneton thinks so. She has Prefect here all made up for a date. We think there'll be a test drive today.
Prefect	Oh I do hope it's a nice man who can afford to look after me.

Anglia	As long as it isn't Mr Dent.
Rod	Mr Dent? Why?
Anglia	Mr Dent is an elderly local man who likes old model cars, but he gets little dings and scratches in carparks, You know how they all hurt. Some need beatings.
Prefect	Beatings?!
Anglia	Yes, panel beating. Eventually the cars are written off by his insurance company. Then he trades them in for a well-kept old car, and starts all over again. . . . death by a thousand dings.
Prefect	I couldn't bear that. Mr Sparkle would turn over in his grave.
Anglia (*panicked*)	Uh no! Look who's coming! It's him. Mr Dent himself! And he's heading towards us. Oh no!
Prefect	He must be my test drive. Ooh! I'm getting hot flushes again. He's scary.
(pause)	
Rod	Hey, he's turned away – heading for the poor Cortina.
Prefect	Oh, poor Tina. She's hardly had a scratch in her life. Oh dear, she's in for some pain.
Rod	You're lucky, old girl. For all your pride, good owners have a prejudice for youth, power and a bit of style. You miss out on all three counts.

Prefect turns her nose up, scoffing.

Rod	Hey, you guys, How long does Mrs Benneton keep you before sending you to the auctions or the wreckers?
Prefect	I don't know. I've only been here 4 weeks, but I think Mrs Benneton is fond of me. She'll find me a good home.
Anglia	Prefect, don't be so naïve. Used car salespeople don't get fond of cars. They just want to move them.
Prefect	She wouldn't let me go to a wrecker.
Rod	I think Anglia's right. Your time is up. She'll send you to the auctions, and a wrecker will buy you <u>there</u>. I know you're good for your age, but you're out of date, babe. Nobody wants us with no modern electronics, no power, and huge doctors' bills.
Prefect	What a cynic you are.
Rod	Hey, babe, I was lucky. You need major surgery to survive – a strip down, sand blast and re-build. I've been through it all. Now I'm on magazine covers.
Anglia	You're even older than us. Don't you have stiff joints? I do.

Rod	Hey, stiff can be good . . . I've had my suspension stiffened. A squirt of oil on your joints and you could be on the street again.
Prefect	On the street. How nice. I'd like to be a working girl again.
Rod	You could, you could. You just need a buyer who will put in the hours – and the dollars.
Prefect	I'd like a buyer like Mr Sparkle. Someone to really love me.
Rod	Good luck, old girl, but I think you're past it. It's a shame old Mr Dent wasn't interested.
Prefect	Who would buy you? Not an original bone in your body. No class. Noisy. Black!
Rod	People are into black these days
Anglia	I'd be happy with anyone – except a wrecker.
Prefect	You're just a slut . . . Look, there's a nice young girl coming over. I bet her father has offered her a first car to take to University.
Anglia	Huh, I bet she will never wash you or change your oil or anything.
Prefect	Who cares? She'll love my good looks and my gentle nature. Watch my dust, guys.

Prefect struts away, looking very pleased with herself.

Anglia	There she goes. Looks like a marriage made in heaven.
Rod	I don't think so, Anglia.
Anglia	What do you mean? She looks like a sweet kid. Prefect can get by for years without washing or servicing.
Rod	Oh, she'll be serviced alright. I know the girl from the car club. They call her Bev the Banger.
Anglia	Oh, she's a bit promiscuous, is she?
Rod	No, she has only one interest – to win the Collins Cup.
Anglia	Donated by Mr Collins, that awful man who owns the Panel Beating Business?
Rod	Yes. She's a demolition derby champion. She's the most aggressive, vicious driver on the circuit, and she's gunning for the new Collins Class – for 1950s technology, and less than 1000cc. Prefect's about to be stripped, bored out, and head shaved.
Anglia	Oh dear. She won't like that.
Rod	You bet.
Anglia	Well, as Mrs Benneton says, there's a buyer out there for everyone. Not many Mr Darcys, but beggars can't be choosers.

Rod   I think we'll meet up at the wreckers soon. At least it's less painful than demolition derbies . . . and weekly beatings.

The cars shudder and "deflate".

END

Jane Austen's **Pride and Prejudice** ILLUSTRATED, BRIEFLY by Jen Sorensen

"IT IS A TRUTH UNIVERSALLY ACKNOWLEDGED, THAT A SINGLE MAN IN POSSESSION OF A GOOD FORTUNE MUST BE IN WANT OF A WIFE."

MAIN PLAYERS

ELIZABETH BENNET	JANE BENNET	MRS. BENNET	MR. BENNET	MR. BINGLEY	MR. DARCY	MR. COLLINS
A SHARP AND SELF-POSSESSED YOUNG WOMAN	HER BEAUTIFUL OLDER SISTER	THEIR MOTHER, EAGER TO MARRY OFF HER DAUGHTERS TO WEALTHY MEN	HER WRY HUSBAND	AFFABLE ARISTOCRAT. COURTS JANE	DASHING BUT ARROGANT ARISTOCRAT	MR. BENNET'S COUSIN AND HEIR

The real cars, the basis for the play – Anglia hotrod, Ford Anglia, Ford Prefect.

NOT AGAIN!

Written and presented at Bundanoon in 2014. It won its heat and was selected for Sydney Short & Sweet (Top 80), Sydney. Miranda Lean played Judy, Thomas-Andrew Baxter played Steve, and David O'Halloran was Col.

Lorelei Tait directed the show at Short & Sweet.

NOT AGAIN!

A Ten-minute Play by Brian Haydon

Cast:

Steve, mid-thirties, mild-mannered, has just been beaten up.

Judy, a thirty-ish married woman.

Col, Judy's husband, arrogant, tough; a salesman.

Scene 1 - *a park.*

Steve crawls across stage, in pain, spitting blood, groaning, mumbling.

Enter Judy, walking in the park. She sees Steve, rushes to his aid.

Judy:	Oh my God, are you alright?
Steve:	Not really. I think my ribs are broken, and I can't see.
Judy:	I'll get an ambulance.
Steve:	No. They'll kill me.
Judy:	Who?
Steve:	The guys who beat me up.
Judy:	Why?
Steve:	It was a gang. One of them said I insulted his girlfriend. urrgh.

Judy: It can be dangerous in this park.

*Steve chokes, coughs, has his hands between his legs as he
rolls onto his side.*

Judy: Is your hand hurt too?

Steve: No. they kicked me in the nuts.

Judy: I can only imagine. You poor thing. Let me
               wipe your face.

She takes a tissue from her purse and wipes his face.

Judy: There's a cut over your eye, and . . . Oh,
               dear, your teeth. And a shiner! Are you sure
               an ambulance is out of the question?

Steve: Yes, they are probably watching.

Judy looks around.

Judy: I can't see anyone.

Steve: Please! Urrgh.

Judy: Look, I live just off the park. I can clean you
               up there. Do you think you can walk?

Steve: I'll try. Thank you so much. I'm Steve.

Judy: I'm Judy. Let's go. Easy, now.

Steve struggles to his feet. His hand is still between his legs. Judy supports him as he staggers offstage with her. Blackout.

*Lights up on **new scene**, the interior of Judy's Apartment.*

They enter, Judy supporting him, Steve is still groaning and weak.

Judy: I'll get some washers and towels.

Steve: I'm sorry to bother you.

Steve sits on a chair, obviously in pain. Judy exits and returns with towels, a glass of water and a Panadol. She wipes his head. He still has his hands between his legs.

Judy: Here, take a Panadol.

Steve: Thank you. You're so kind.

Judy: You're pretty bruised, but I don't think you've broken any bones. How do your ribs feel?

Steve: Ok now. It's just my . . .

Judy: Testicles?

Steve: Yes. He . . . They kicked me there over and over.

Judy: How many of them were there?

Steve:	I don't know. I couldn't see after my eye was split.
Judy:	Was it a gang?
Steve:	I've never seen them before.
Judy:	You'd better report it to the police.
Steve:	God, no. They warned me against that.
Judy:	Were you dealing drugs or something?
Steve:	No, I'm just an accountant. I live over on the other side of the park.
Judy:	Alone?
Steve:	No, I'm . . . Well, I used to be . . . Married.
Judy:	What do you mean, used to be?
Steve:	We were married for five years, but one day recently I came home and found her in bed with another man. They just laughed at me and carried on. I think the marriage is kaput.
Judy:	Oh, you poor thing. You really are in the wars, aren't you ! Do you feel up to a glass of wine?
Steve:	I need one, please. And you?
Judy:	Oh yes, I'll have one too.
Steve:	No, I meant are you married?
Judy:	Oh yes, my husband's a salesman. We get on OK. He's been away for a few days. He'll be back today.

Judy fetches two glasses of wine.

Judy:	So did you move out or did your wife? Or are you still together?
Steve:	Well, ah . . . .
Judy:	How long since you caught her in bed with this guy?
Steve:	Just recently. I . . . I've sort of moved out.
Judy:	Sort of?
Steve:	I don't know who will move out, or if we'll stay together. *Pause*. Look, I think I'd better tell you the full story. . . It only happened today. Just before I met you in the park. I went home early, and heard the sounds in the bedroom. I was tempted to sneak out, but . . . I thought I'd face up to the situation, show a little indignation, scare the guy out, let my wife beg for forgiveness. Anyhow, they saw me come into the bedroom, and just kept at it. When they finished, I suggested it might be proper for the man to leave, now.
Judy:	That was very polite of you.
Steve:	Yes, but the guy jumped out of bed and laid into me. He was naked, but he fought like a madman, as if HE was the wronged party. I lashed out and kicked him where it hurts,

but that just enraged him. He knocked me down and kicked me, over and over again. He kept saying he would kick my balls into my throat.

Judy: So there was no gang?

Steve: No, there wasn't a gang, but it felt like one. Cruel bastard, though. I'm sorry I lied.

Judy: What are you going to do now?

Steve: I don't know. I can't go home. He may be still there. He warned me against talking to the police or anyone else.

Judy: Do you think he'll stay with your wife, then?

Steve: Who knows. I had no idea it was going on.

Steve groans again.

Judy: What is it?

Steve: My balls. They ache like hell. Maybe he <u>has</u> kicked them into my throat.

Judy: Look, I used to be a nurse, so I'm not embarrassed. Why don't you loosen your pants.

Steve stands up and drops his trousers to his knees but leaves his underpants on. He groans.

Judy:	Is that better?
Steve:	I think so.
Judy:	Any bleeding?
Steve:	I don't think so.
Judy:	Let me just check.

Judy drops to her knees, and is looking for bleeding when the door bursts open and Col enters.

Col:	Hi, Jude, I need a . . . What the hell?

Judy springs to her feet. Steve pulls up his trousers.

Steve:	Oh no!
Judy:	It's not whatever you're thinking, Col. This poor man has just been beaten up after he caught his wife with another man.
Col:	There seems to be quite a bit of it going on in this neighbourhood.
Judy:	I was just checking his injuries to see if he needs a doctor.
Col:	Oh yes, just like those massage parlours down the road. "Let us relieve all your pain and tension".
Judy:	Don't be silly. You could show a little sympathy too.

Col:	Sympathy? A man comes home from a hard day's work and finds his wife . . . on her knees . . . being a slut.

Steve groans, obviously still in pain.

Judy:	Look, I was just being a good Samaritan. The man needed help
Col:	Yes, of course. Hence the wine, the towels, you on your knees . . . and him moaning in ecstasy.
Judy:	You know I don't play around.
Col:	This doesn't look like playing. This looks like working. Are you that desperate for money? Or just for sex? A little bit of a business on the side . . . or on your knees . . . while I was away, eh?
Judy:	Don't be ridiculous.
Col:	Is this the best you can do? This creep? He must have paid you a lot. How much <u>do</u> you charge, anyway? Eh?
Judy:	I've never had an affair or . . .
Col:	Bullshit ! Having an affair is one thing. You'd only have it off with weasels like this if you were charging. . *(PAUSE)* Well thanks for the freebies. I really appreciate <u>my</u> family discount.
Steve:	I've got to go.

Col:	No you don't, buster. I've got a job to finish with you.
Judy:	What do you mean?
Col:	Shut up, bitch.
Steve:	I won't say anything, I swear.
Col:	I don't care how much you paid my wife. You're going to pay through the nose – and throat.
Judy:	Leave him alone, Col, he's just a little guy.
Col:	He's a rat. He's gonna be sorry.

Col chases Steve, but Steve escapes through the door as Col trips on the chair.

Judy blocks the door, but Col throws her across the room. Col looks out the door, but can't see Steve. Col calls out to him.

Col:	Come back and fight like a man, you weasel. I'll kick your balls into your throat.

Col storms out.

Judy:	NO!

Judy howls and collapses.

END

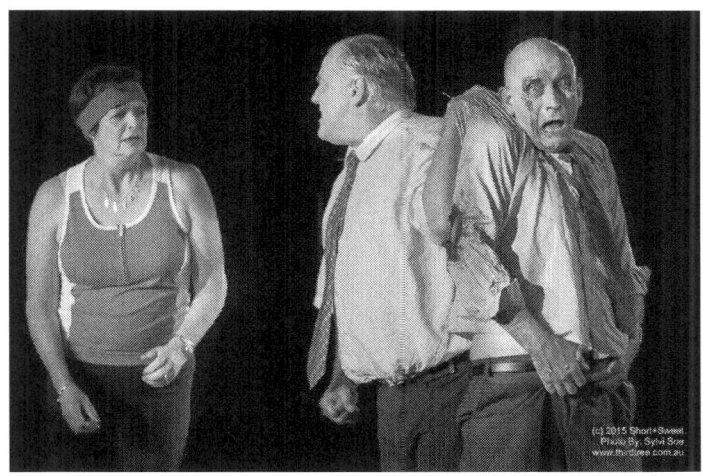

Tension at Short & Sweet, Sydney

All through history
Meetings by chance have produced
Serendipity.

Brian Haydon

DISTAIN

Distain won the Judge's prize at its heat of Sydney Crash Test Drama, benefiting from two excellent actors. The idea arose from the notion of a stark white tablecloth being progressively stained with blood-red wine as a relationship collapsed. Here is the report from Sydney CTD.

May 9, 2016 Heat CTD

Distain, *written by Brian Haydon and directed by Bryan McMahon. Solid performances by Allan Long as Willy and Kate Bookallil as Zola saw this great play* <u>win Best Actress Runner Up</u> *for Kate as well as the* <u>Judge's Choice for Best Play</u>! **Distain** *wins a spot in the Crash Test Drama finals in July!*

Allan & Kate, CTD Heat Sydney

I conducted many experiments with red food colouring and a starched white sheet to get the effect, but for the performance I over-filled the wine glass, and the imitation red wine spilled on the floor. After the play I had to quickly mop the floor. The effect on the table-cloth was excellent.

I was unable to attend rehearsals for the final, but two actors offered to self-direct with a friend. Here is the report.

July 2016 Finals CTD SYD

Distain, *written by Brian Haydon and directed by Halina Abramowicz. It starred Marisa Newnes as Zola and Bobby Babin as Willy.*

Bobby and Marisa at Sydney CTD Final

This play has never been presented at Bundanoon Crash Test Drama, but I offered the script to an acting workshop conducted by Noeleen Brown at Bowral. Only parts were read, but it gave opportunities for many variations in the acting. With no other male actors attending, I had to read the male part several times, and Noeleen wholeheartedly agreed with my assertion that I am no actor.

DISTAIN

A ten-minute play by Brian Haydon

Characters
Zola, a woman in her late 30s
Willy, her second husband, late 30s early 40s

Scene
The stage is bare except for a small table, covered by a pure white starched tablecloth, on which is a single glass and a bottle of red wine.

Enter Zola

Zola (to audience):   I knew I'd get it right second time around. My new husband is kind, considerate, and generous. More important, he adores me!

Enter Willy.

Willy: Hi, hon, how's the love of my life?

Zola: She just can't wait to get her hands on you, you gorgeous hunk.

Willy: Well, she'll just have to wait a little while. She should grab her coat. We need to celebrate the hunk's promotion at work.

Zola: Whee! Congratulations. Does that mean I can afford a new pair of shoes?

Willy: You can afford a whole new wardrobe. They made me a partner.

Zola pours some wine, and takes a sip.

Zola (to audience):   That night was simply wonderful. Willy was really turned on, and we came home and . . . cavorted until we were worn out.

Willy (to audience):   Zola was hot. I mean really hot. Not just good looking, although she had a great body, a way of moving it, and those sparkling eyes that dwelt on me. She was really turned on that night. So was I. It was magic. That was nearly a year ago now.

Zola: Will you be home early tonight, Willy? It is our anniversary, and I have a special meal prepared.

Willy: Ah, I think so.

Zola: What do you mean, you think so?

Willy: You know Mr Goldberg is my biggest client. He wants to take me to lunch to discuss a big new merger he is planning.

Zola: Well, that's lunch. I'm talking about dinner . . . and afters.

Willy: I'll be there, Zola. After all, Mr Goldberg is only our meal ticket. You're my meal.

They cuddle briefly.

Zola: I love it when you talk dirty. I'll have the champagne on ice from 6:30 and the caviar starter ready at 7:30. It could be a late night.

Zola sips the wine.

Zola (to audience):   That anniversary celebration night was a disaster. Willy came home drunk and worn out. He barely touched his dinner, and staggered off to bed. There was no dessert that night, at the table or in bed.

Zola fills the glass.

Willy (to audience):   Zola was really pissed off that night. She was in a funk for days. She was unreasonable, and didn't want to hear about the big deal I had secured with Mr Goldberg.

Zola: Well, if we couldn't celebrate our wedding anniversary, would you be available to celebrate the anniversary of your promotion to partner last year? I know you have important clients to entertain, but can they compete with our epic celebration 365 days ago?

Willy: No way. That's sacred. I want to re-enact that every year for the next 50 years.

Zola: We'll see.

Willy (to audience):   When I got home, Zola was wobbly. She couldn't stand up, and she was slurring her words. The food was burnt, and she was all over me like a rash, but somehow it wasn't a turn-on.

Zola pours more wine into the glass, and spills some on the tablecloth.

Zola (to audience):   Willy was rude to me that night. I was just a little tipsy. I wanted to really please him with some experimental hanky-panky. I didn't realise he was such a prude. He wasn't even into kissing, let alone what I had planned.

Willy (to audience)   : Zola had gone out and bought all this fancy underwear. Lace, with holes everywhere. Her boobs were nudging her chin. The split in her skirt meant that there was no mystery left. I was thinking about the company function next week, where her 6 inch heels and scarlet lipstick would be regarded as . . . well, whorish. She thought it would turn me on, God bless her, but it had the opposite effect.

Zola pours some more wine, spilling quite a bit.

Zola: Willy, tell me honestly. Are you having an affair?

Willy: What? Of course not. What makes you think that?

Zola: Well, they say that the first sign is loss of libido with your wife.

Willy: Did they also say that stress and fatigue can have the same effect?

Zola: Yes, but that's avoidable. It's just a matter of priorities.

Zola spills some more wine.

Willy (to audience): I started having suspicions that Zola was the one having a bit on the side. She had started a job at the local restaurant, where all these over-confident sales types took their clients for lunch. Of course, they showed off by flirting and showing their familiarity with the waitress. I was too busy to care much.

Zola pours some more wine.

Zola (to audience): I was starting to feel depressed. I was neglected. There was no fun in my life except when we occasionally went out with friends. When I got my job, it was suddenly exciting. Friendly customers, and these good looking young chaps flirting with me. It made me feel good, but I kept my head.

Willy: I have to go away for three days next week. Big deal coming up.

Zola: Oh! Are you going alone?

Willy: No, Alice will be coming. She has to take all the notes and type up the contracts.

Zola: Is Alice the blonde bimbo with the fluttering eyelashes?

Willy: No . . . well, I hadn't noticed really. It's just work. We do it every day.

Zola: Hmm. A pity you don't do it every day at home.

Willy: Look, you know I'm too sensible to jeopardise our marriage, let alone with someone from work.

Zola: That's what they all say.

Willy: We'll have separate rooms. It's pure business.

Zola: Pure monkey business more likely. Will you have meals together?

Willy: Yes, but mostly with the clients.

Zola: And drinks before, during and after?

Willy: Trust me, Zola. I can handle it.

Zola sips some wine.

Zola (to audience):   Trust him! Every night I lay awake imagining Willy and the bimbo drunk and snuggled up in that hotel. I wasn't going to give him the satisfaction of calling him He would just say it was a late night negotiating, anyway.

Willy (to audience):   There was nothing I could do to convince Zola. I hadn't noticed how attractive Alice was till then, but she behaved professionally, and I nipped any temptation in the bud.

Zola: So, was the bimbo able to keep her paws off you?

Willy: She did her job and I did mine. No flirting, no touching. It didn't even come up.

Zola: You must be feeling <u>very</u> fatigued and stressed.

Zola pours more wine – mostly onto the tablecloth.

Zola *(to audience)*:   I was really upset. Thinking of Willy sharing hotels with that Alice. The third time they went away, I had a drink before work, and for the first time gave my mobile number to a guy who was always flirting with me.

Willy *(to audience)*:   Zola couldn't believe that there was nothing between Alice and me. Sure, I sometimes found myself studying her walk – almost leering, but I told myself my career is too important, and these days a slight lapse and you're accused of sexual harassment, and that's it, guilty or not.

Zola: We haven't been discussing our relationship lately.

Willy: We don't need to, do we? Is anything wrong?

Zola: My biological clock is ticking away, you know.

Willy: Are you pregnant?

Zola: No, but I'd like to be.

Willy: You're right. We haven't discussed that. Let's make babies.

Zola pours some wine. He cuddles her, but she disengages.

Zola: You're so romantic. If we just . . . made love, it would happen.

Willy: I think you're drinking a little too much.

Zola: I think you're wearing yourself out with the bimbo on "business" trips.

Zola pours more wine. The tablecloth is now badly stained down the front.

Willy *(to audience)*:   I didn't think it would happen. But it did. Zola was pregnant. I was worried about foetal alcohol syndrome. All I could do was try to dry her out.

Zola pours more wine on the tablecloth, which is becoming soaked.

Zola *(to audience):*   I hope he doesn't ask for DNA testing. There's no way it's his. Once I realised, I seduced him a few times. It wasn't that hard. Well, you know what I mean. There were two clients at the café who could be the father. If they knew they'd run a mile, I think.

Willy: You seem to be blooming, Zola. There's a real glow about you.

Zola: I guess this is what I was made for.

Willy: You will go easy on the booze, won't you!

Zola: You look after your side. Cut down on those trips with the bimbo. Our child will need a father being around, not sleeping around.

Willy (to audience):   You know, I'm not sure I'm ready for this father business. I mean, a baby is not just for Christmas. It's nice making them, but I can see trouble brewing.

Zola (to audience):   You know, I don't even like him anymore. I don't like to sleep with him. I don't want him to touch me. I'll have to stick it out for the baby, though.

Willy: Darling, my boss has invited us to cocktails tomorrow night. Are you up for it?

Zola: I'm sorry, darling. I'll be too tired. And I'm not drinking these days, you know. . . but don"t worry, Alice will be there (*sarcastic*).

Willy: No, she's resigned. Apparently she's pregnant.

Zola: Apparently!

Both roll their eyes and exit. Blackout.

END

THE HUNDRED-DOLLAR BILL

In March 2019, this play was crash tested at Bundanoon. Charlie was played by Richard Bosley-Craft, Bert by Ron Russell. I am still searching for the ladies.

THE HUNDRED DOLLAR BILL
A Ten-Minute Play by Brian Haydon

Scene 1 - a kitchen table with 2 chairs

Scene 2 – an Accountant's office, 2 chairs opposite each other across a table

Scene 3 - A psychiatrist's Room

Scene 4 – a hairdressing salon.

Cast:

Abigail, a housewife in scene 1, who turns out to be a hairdresser in Scene 4

Charlie, a handyman

Bert, an accountant

Donna, a counsellor.

Scene 1: *Abi and Charlie sit at a kitchen table, facing each other. Charlie stage left.*

Abi:	Oh, thank you Charlie. That tap has been leaking for weeks, and the sink looked like overflowing.
Charlie:	No prob, Missus. And thanks for the cuppa. Just what I needed.
Abi:	That's the least I can do. It's such a relief.
Charlie:	Y'know, I don't mind the call-out at all – I need the money, y'know. But your husband should be able to do such simple jobs.
Abi:	God, no. He's hopeless hopeless! He has a workshop full of tools, and a shelf of

204

handyman manuals, and he can barely change a light globe.

Charlie: Well, we each have our little lot in life, y'know. I was lucky. My old man was a mechanic. We fixed cars so we had to do a bit of plumbing and electrical, y'know.

Abi: My husband can wash and vacuum his car. That's about it. He's hopeless. We spend a fortune on repairs and servicing. Hopeless!

Charlie: I can't do so much these days, y'know. The cars are run by computers. Can't even tune the carby, y'know. Bloody computers! I don't understand 'em either, Missus.

Abi: Well, at least Bert is pretty good with computers. He taps away all night. Can't help me when I have a problem though. Hopeless!

Charlie: Y'know, you're lucky in a way. I bet he can tune in the stations on your TV.

Abi: Oh yes, and he can change the batteries in the remote, and turn the modem off and on when it fails, but find my lost files? Hopeless.

Charlie: Well, missus, I'd best be going. Thanks for the cuppa. I'll just grab me tools. (*he stands*)

Abi: (*she stands*) Can you send me an invoice? I can get Bert to pay you online.

Charlie: It's only a hundred and fifty dollars, y'know. A hundred if you pay me cash.

Abi fossicks in her purse (or biscuit tin!) and produces a hundred-dollar bill.

Abi: You don't see many of <u>these!</u>

She hands it to him.

Charlie: Thanks, Missus. Wow, a hundred dollar bill! I don't see many of these either, y'know. You can call me any time. Here's the number.

He gives her a business card; she waves and exits stage right.

Charlie moves his chair for the next scene, slightly out then back in.

Enter Bert (R).

Bert: Ah, Mister Cooper.

Charlie: Ah, g'day.

They shake hands, then sit. Charlie is at stage left again, Bert stage R.

Bert: How's business going?

Charlie: There's plenty of work, but I can't seem to get ahead, y'know. What do you make of the books?

Bert:	Oh dear! As you say, you aren't accumulating much of a nest egg. You seem to break even each year, but at least you own your van.
Charlie:	That's the main thing, y'know.
Bert:	I don't know how you manage, with so little income.
Charlie:	Oh, y'know, the odd pokie wins, and the lottery winnings (*winks*). A mate at the pub gives me some great tips on the nags, y'know.
Bert:	Oh dear. Mr Cooper, I'm not selling insurance or superannuation funds, but do you realise you have no life insurance, and no superannuation savings.
Charlie:	Yes, but no tax to pay, and no kids, y'know. I can pay my shout at the pub.
Bert:	Oh dear! But what about retirement?
Charlie:	I'll never retire. What would I do? I'd get the pension, y'know.
Bert:	Oh dear! Do you know how much pensioners earn?
Charlie:	No, but they get lots of discounts, y'know.
Bert:	Oh dear. But what about your wife? How would she survive if you had an accident?
Charlie:	She makes more money than me, y'know. She pays the mortgage, and the cleaner, and the grocer bil .

Bert:	You're a lucky man, Mr Cooper.
Charlie:	Between you and me, she likes to have me in the sack, y'know. Can't stand wimps. Loves a bit of . . . growling, if you know what I mean.
Bert:	Oh dear. Lucky you. What does she do for a living?
Charlie:	She's some sort of a shrink, I think. An anulyst, but I don't know what she anulises, y'know. Comes home randy as . .
Bert:	Oh dear! I think I understand, Mr Cooper. Now, you don't need a tax return at this stage, so I can't charge you my normal fee. A hundred dollars will do. You can pay online if you like.
Charlie:	Nar, don't be silly. I'll pay cash.

Charlie takes a (large) hundred dollar bill from his pocket and hands it to Bert.

Bert holds it up to the light, used to checking for counterfeits.

Bert:	Oh dear! A hundred dollar bill! You don't see many of these. I only use plastic, myself. Thanks.

Exit Charlie (L). Bert moves his chair to the next scene, out and in again stage R. Enter Donna.(L)

Donna:	Hello, Bert.
Bert:	Hi, Doctor Carlson
Donna:	Hmm. I think after 6 sessions you can call me by first name. Call me Donna.
Bert:	O.K, Dr Carlson . . mean Donna. Oh Dear!

They both sit, Bert reclining on couch, if available.

Donna:	Hmm. Last session we were working on self-esteem. How are the exercises going, hmm?
Bert:	Oh dear! No problem in reminding myself of my good points – that doesn't take long. Oh dear! Not long at all.
Donna:	Hmm. And the self-development exercises?
Bert:	I'm doing the push-ups every day. My wife laughs at me. Oh Dear. She suggests I do them in bed!
Donna:	Hmm!
Bert:	I've stopped reading computer and accounting books, and I'm reading women's magazines, . . . surreptitiously of course. Oh dear! They are strange creatures. All emotion and no logic from what I can gather.
Donna:	Hmm! And TV viewing?

Bert:	I took your advice and started watching with my wife, whatever she chooses. Oh dear. Dancing competitions, reality TV, and costume dramas . . . with lots of adultery and bonking, it seems. Oh dear!
Donna:	Has she noticed the new, considerate, compassionate, caring you?
Bert:	I don't think that's what she wants. Oh dear. She seems to get excited, sort of, by the villains, the cruel, nasty bullies. Oh dear. I'm confused.
Donna:	Hmm! I see you have a new haircut.
Bert:	Yes! I look in the mirror and see a new man. Oh dear. Still a wimp, but a new man.
Donna:	Hmm! Well that's the first step to self-esteem. Change! Keep up the good work, Bert. I think the next step should be, hmm, a small dose of masculinity. Hmm. Think about it, and we'll discuss your thoughts next week.
Bert:	Thanks, Dr Carlson . . oh dear . .I mean Donna. Do you still prefer cash? A hundred dollars?
Donna:	Hmm *(affirmative)*

He hands her a hundred dollar bill. She rolls it in her hand.

Exit Bert (R).

Donna: Hmm! You don't see many of these. A real
                hundred dollar bil .

Donna turns her chair around and downstage, and sits.
Enter Abi (R) sweeping the floor.

Abi: Oh, Hi, Donna. How are you? Nice day
                today. No trouble parking?

Abi stands behind Donna, they face an imaginary mirror

Donna: Hi, Abi. I'm well thanks. Yes, it's fine
                outside. Hmm. What was the other
                question?

Abi: Ah, my memory is hopeless. Greeting,
                weather, . . . oh yes, parking.

Donna: `Hmm. Not bad. How are you? Love your
                blouse.

Abi: Oh, I'm fine thanks. What was the other
                question?

Donna: Hmm. Your blouse.

Abi: Oh yes, I didn't have anything to match my
                new nail polish. It was hopeless, and this
                was just right. Now for the shoes to match.

Donna: Oh, it's hard to be a woman. Men just don't
                understand.

Abi: Hopeless. They wear the same thing every
                day, don't notice our carefully selected
                wardrobes, and never look after their nails.

211

Both:	YUK!
Abi:	What would you like today? Are you due for a change?
Donna:	I need a change – a change of mood, a change of lifestyle, mm, a change of husband . . .
Abi:	What, are you having problems? Has he been playing up?
Donna:	Hmm, you're joking. No physically all is good. Very good. It's the intellectual side. We can't have a decent conversation. He's full of confidence, but hmm he doesn't realise his weaknesses. Or my intellectual frustration.
Abi:	So going blonde won't work. And I know you don't like strong colours or streaks.
Donna:	Hmm, and I don't want to look like a librarian.
Abi:	What about a radical geometric cut?
Donna:	Hmm! I don't know how he would take that.
Abi:	We are hopeless! Why would anyone have their haircut for a man? Especially when you're married?
Donna:	You're right. Hmm. So who do we dress for?
Abi:	Other women, of course. Only our girlfriends notice any change, and dole out the compliments, and ask who your hairdresser is, and what it cost.

Donna:	Hmm. Would a bob be too big a change?
Abi:	Not right for your nose. And your expensive earrings would disappear.
Donna:	Hmm. I'm not ready for a "sensible" haircut yet.
Abi:	No. Plenty of time for that when you're older
Donna:	Hmm. Well leave it long and just trim the ends. Charlie likes me to . . .
Abi:	We're not dressing for Charlie, remember?
Donna:	Right. Oh, is it OK f I give you a hundred dollar bill today? It's all I have.
Abi:	That's fine.

Donna pays Abi in advance; Abi rolls the note between her fingers.

Abi:	You don't see these very often.

She puts it in her pocket and gets her scissors ready

Donna:	Mmm. Not too short, now.

Blackout

END

Ron and Richard as Bert and Charlie at CTD Bundanoon

THE BOYFRIEND

This play was first read at Bundanoon Crash Test Drama in 2019. It was a finalist, and in the final won the audience vote qualifying for Sydney Short & Sweet 2020, where it ran its season before the festival was called off because of the COVID Pandemic. The original cast of Rebecca Howarth as Rose and Ruth Smoother as Paula played in all the performances.

THE BOYFRIEND
A Ten-Minute Play by Brian Haydon

Cast:

Paula.   30 ish, lives with her mother

Rose.   55 ish, Paula's mother

Scene: The Living Room of a modest suburban house. Stage left is a hallway to the front door, stage right a hallway leading to the rest of the house.

INTRO MUSIC – "My Guy", by Mary Wells.

Rose is sitting at a table, fuming.

LIGHTS UP, MUSIC DOWN

Enter Paula.

Paula: Hi, Mum. How are you?

Rose: I was OK until the beef burnt. You said you'd be here at 6.

Paula: Sorry, Mum. I had a client come in just before closing time.

Rose: Bah! Some people are just so inconsiderate.

Paula: We couldn't afford to lose a client, Mum. she came straight from work. She wasn't really being inconsiderate.

Rose: I wasn't talking about her. I was talking about you. Are these customers more important than your Mum?

Paula: Of course not, Mum, but we have to be a bit flexible sometimes.

Rose: That's ripe. You lecturing me about flexibility. All these years, raising you to be tolerant, and to not over-commit, and to treat people with digni . . .

Paula: I know Mum. I try to live up to all you've taught me. And I do love you, Mum.

She gives her a hug.

Paula: Would you like a sherry?

Rose: Don't go thinking that alcohol will soften the hurt.

Paula pours a sherry and opens a beer for herself, gives her mother the sherry and takes a swig of the beer herself.

Rose: Do you have to drink like a wharfie? We do have glasses, you know.

Paula: I know, Mum, but I'm really thirsty. It's been a hard day.

Rose: Hard day! Sitting in an air-conditioned office, chatting with clients and playing with your computer.

Paula: You're right that it's not taxing physically, but the stress, Mum, it tires you out as much as any labouring work.

Rose (*sarcastically*): Oh, you poor thing. I used to work 10 hours a day, six days a week in two jobs, just to make ends meet, and Cart you around with me until you started school. Then you finished school, and I thought ah, at last. She'll get a job, and I can relax.

Paula: I know Mum, and I appreciate it.

Rose: But no, you went off to University, double degree and a master of marching in demonstrations.

Paula: I did work as a waitress all that time, Mum.

Rose: Sure, and all the money went on parties and booze, and fashionable jeans with holes in them.

Paula: That's Uni, Mum. I had to pay rent, and eat, too,

Rose: So what happened to this new boyfriend?

Paula: Just parking the bike, Mum.

Rose: Bike?

Paula: Yes, there were no parking spaces in the whole
        street.

Rose: Bike! Two wheels! So he can't afford a car?

Paula: I don't know that it's a matter of affordability,
        Mum.

Rose: Anyone worth his salt can afford a car.

Paula: Did I say it was a "he" Mum?

Rose: WHAT? You've turned into a . . .
Paula: Just kidding, Mum

Rose: That's not funny. I just saw my whole life pass
        before my eyes. No wedding, no grandchildren, the
        shame of facing the church auxiliary, having to build
        an extension for an extra visitor's room . . .

Paula: Why an extra visitor's room?

Rose: I'm not having you doing all those (*she shudders*) in
        my house.

Paula: Oh Mum, you are. . .

Rose: What? Old fashioned? Moral?

Paula: It's not worth arguing about, Mum. It's hypothetical.

Rose: Don't go confusing me with your technical terms.

Paula: Sorry, Mum.

Rose: So he is a "He"?

Paula: Absolutely, Mum. Fully equipped; deep voiced.

Rose: I knew you would score a real man. I bet he is tall, dark, with a twinkle in his eye. Just like your dear papa was. But unlike your father a professional; caring . . . generous . . .

Paula: Oh, Mum. You and your fantasies. Life isn't a Mills and Boon novel.

Rose: Oh, I'm past reading romantic books.

Paula: I'm glad, Mum.

Rose: No, now I'm into reality TV. I have an extended family.

Paula: Good, Mum. Are you still flirting with Mr Goldstein next door?

Rose: No, he found a tart. She hung around; false eyelashes like a camel: big hair wig,

Paula   False (her hands cup her breasts)?

Rose: No, Maurice would always know the real thing.

Paula: I don't know Mum. The fa sies are pretty good these days. They look so real.

Rose: Maurice isn't one for visual inspection, if you know what I mean.

Paula: I think I know. What about the tart?

Rose: What do you mean?

Paula: Is she scintillating company? Cultured?

Rose: I don't know. I haven't met her. I've smelt her.

Paula: Smelt her?

Rose: Yes. She leaves a cloud of cologne right along the street.

Paula: I think I know the type. Make-up applied with a trowel?

Rose: Yas! Probably takes two hours to put it on and another hour to take it off each night.

Paula: And tight skirts?

Rose: She must take hours to get into them, too.

Paula: What about heels?

Rose: Oh, at least three and a half inches. I'm waiting for her to stumble on Maurice's doorstep.

Paula: Looks like "no contest", Mum, if that's what appeals to Maurice.

Rose: Can you believe, he bought himself a red sports car.

Paula: That's the last resort of the involuntarily celibates.

Pause - They take a drink.

Rose: He's probably spending a fortune on Viagra.

Paula: Is he still around?

Rose: They were off on a world cruise, last I heard.

Rose: What does this new boyfriend do for a living? Is he a lawyer like you? He is well off, isn't he?

Paula: I wouldn't say that, Mum.

Rose: An ABC journalist?

Paula: That's an oxymoron, Mum.

Rose: I'm sure he's no moron if you are interested in him. No, he must be an intellectual of some sort. A Professor? A scientist?

Paula: No, I'm not into geeks.

Rose: Don't tell me he's one of those crusty old judges, or creaky old magistrates.

Paula: Mum! I wouldn't want a geriatric, no matter how rich.

Rose: A Tradesman with his own business? No, he'd be driving a ute.

A sports star, an actor?

Paula: Getting warm.

Rose: He's on Masterchef! Oh no, he'll pick my meal to bits!

Paula: No, Mum, closer to home.

Rose: Is he . . . (*Local celebrity*)? *** TBA

Paula: Mum, you have a very low opinion of your daughter

Rose: Alright. I give up.

They take a sip.

Paula: He's an artist!

Rose chokes, spits out her drink.

Rose   Oh no! A long haired, greasy, smelly eccentric weasel with dirty fingernails.

Paula: Mum, where did you get that impression?

Rose: I've seen them on TV. They are usually sex maniacs too.

Paula   Well, what's wrong with that?

Rose: What's wrong with that? Everything. They seduce young innocents, then sling them on the scrap heap. They hardly ever marry their women. They indulge in all sorts of dicey practices. They paint nudes -nearly always female, showing everything - and more!

Paula: More than everything?

Rose: More than is proper.

Paula: There's more to painting than nudes. They usually have a fine sense of colour and light and composition. They create abstract concepts, and they evoke memories and contradictions, and new juxtapositions . . .

Rose   Bullshit! Utter bullshit!

Paula: Have you ever been in a Gallery, or exhibition, Mum?

Rose: Only to support my friends. Elsie Merewether used to do the most beautiful still lifes and landscapes. Her roses were so real looking. And Pearl! Her paintings of bowls of fruit made me hungry. Of course I went to their exhbitions. I bought some. Just to show friendship, and to support them.

Paula: Where are they now, Mum?

Rose: Elsie is dead, and Pearl still wins prizes in the Artarmon Show.

Paula: I mean the paintings. Why aren't they hung here, in the house?

Rose: We changed the colour scheme on the walls. You can't decorate your house round your paintings. Anyway, they didn't try to make a living from their painting.

Paula: No, they sponged off their husbands.

Rose: What's wrong with that.? Men bring home the bacon so their wives can be creative.

Paula: What? How Neanderthal. Before TV the women just made tea cosies and painted flower pots to pass the time.. It was craft, not art.

Rose: Oh, you cretin. They painted, so they are artists. Don't tell me you think flicking paint on a canvas is art. Or putting it through a shredder. Fads. That's all. Something to talk about. Fuel for the hypocrites. Something for the critics to waffle about.

SFX Door knock or doorbell.

Rose, puts down her sherry glass adjusts her hair, adjusts her skirt.

Paula: Are you ready to meet him?

Rose: Of course! . . . ., but I don't have high hopes.

They both head stage left. Paula enters the hallway, then steps back, gesturing as if to say "Voila." Rose looks the boyfriend (who is out of sight in the hallway) up and down.

Rose (*looking out to audience, rolling eyes*):   Ooooh!

They exit left.

BLACKOUT and OUTRO MUSIC – "My Guy" by Mary Wells

END

THE GIRLFRIEND

This play, read at Bundanoon Crash Test Drama in 2019, won no awards, but Anton Baggerman won best actor for his performance as Art, and Wendy Hill read Bev.

The play was a sequel to "The Boyfriend", but it was independent except for a few references.

Aston Martin Launch

THE GIRLFRIEND
A ten-minute play by Brian Haydon

Cast   Art, a 30-ish sculptor of miniatures

Bev, Art's mother

Scene: Art's studio

Art is concentrating on his tiny, intricate sculpture, when his mother walks in.

Bev: Good evening, Art.

Art: Hi, Mum. You're home early. No car sales today?

Bev: No, we have a new model coming out.

Art: Wow, a new Aston Martin DB5, the James Bond car!

He stands, and mimes 007 until he sits down.

A guy in a tux and a chick in a slinky dress and a fur stole?

Bev: That's what we usually do. Bond music, a baddy enters, James Bond spins around and shoots him. Smoke drifts across and the red curtains part to reveal the car and the model. She drapes herself all over him, and they clamber into the car.

Art: It's a good image. The petrol heads drool over the power and acceleration figures . . .the would-be playboys ogle the model - whoah. The accountants calculate the lease figures. the celebrities hired for the occasion are desperately refilling their vodka martinis, shaken, not stirred..

Bev: You've got it figured, Art. You should have been a car salesperson like your mother, instead of going to art school.

Art: Like my father.

Art sits down and continues sculpting.

Bev: You and he are like chalk and cheese. He hardly produced anything. A couple of biscuit tin paintings, a few full-size nudes. I think he slept with almost all the models.

Art: Including you, Mum.

Bev: I was young and naive. And he was an attractive man, your father.

Art: You were a good sort too, Mum. You still look pretty good

Together: For your age.

Bev: We're making a comeback, you know.

Art: What do you mean?

Bev: Society is changing. Women are on the rise.

Art: Of course There are rumours of a female 007!

Bev: Wait till you see our new car. We are appealing to a new breed of Aston Martin buyer – the Superwomen who have smashed through the glass ceiling. They are well-healed, and not just their shoes. They are the predators now.

Art: Come off it, Mum. What sort of woman has that sort of money?

Bev: You'd be surprised, my son.

Art: What, A-list celebrities? Tennis champions? High class escorts?

Bev: Try modern CEOs and self-made millionaires, and hedge fund owners

Art: And heiresses - like Paris Hilton!

Bev: She could be a customer. There's nothing wrong with inheriting an empire.

Art: Have you seen her movies, Mum?

Bev: I don't think so. I didn't realise she was a film star.

Art rolls his eyes.

Art: So they buy an Aston Martin and become cougars?

Bev: So the theory goes.

Art: What's the female equivalent of a sugar-daddy?

Bev   There is none. A woman would never be so crass.

Art   So Mum, have they changed the colour schemes? Are the new cars all shades of pink?

Bev rolls her eyes.

Bev   Well, that would be better than the old shades of grey. No. The new woman wants a classy car, but something to contrast with her red or whiteoutfit with power shoulder pads All white, or all black, with plenty of chrome of course.

Art   And what about the inside?

Bev   Aston Martin did lots of research. They consulted with potential buyers. They want practical things like pedals suitable for high heels. Makeup trays.

Art: I know, lots of internal mirrors, a chill pillow instead of heated seats . . . .

Bev: You just don't understand. They want a dainty little steering wheel, not a macho bicep builder.

Art: I bet they want automatic parking and collision avoidance.

Bev: No, but voice-activated door and window locks to deter undesirables.

Art   Wow! We men could never come up with a list like that. And I'd never expect a woman to buy a performance car.

Bev: They don't give a damn about performance. Just looks, smell, and sound.

Art: I thought only men liked a full-throated exhaust sound.

Bev   But you are such a naïve, sexist, old-fashioned boy.
        . . but I still love you.

        Art looks at his watch.

Art   I'd better get cleaned up. I have a date tonight.

*He wipes his hands on a rag (or his trousers) and runs his
hand through his hair.*

Bev   Aren't you having a shower?

Art   No, Paula gets turned on a bit by the smell of the
        plaster.

Bev   Is this the one with the mother you've been
        dreading to meet? The lawyer lady with the
        impossible mother?

Art   Of course, Mum. We've been going out for about 4
        months now. We get on really well, but her mum is
        a shocker.

Bev: What do you mean, a shocker?

Art: She's really dominant. Thinks she knows everything,
        but she's really old-fashioned. Wants to live her life
        vicariously through her daughter. No man is good
        enough. Especially if he can't change a washer.

Bev: Sounds like your mother.

Art: No, Mum. And she doesn't sound like an Aston
        Martin customer, either.

Bev: It sounds like your girlfriend doesn't give her a good wrap, if that's your only source of information.

Art: Oh, Paula loves her mum. Apparently she's a great cook, and an expert on reality TV.

Bev: Is there a father? What does he do?

Art: No, her father shot through years ago. Couldn't bear the arguments and constant criticism, apparently.

Bev: But that's what husbands are for!

Art: Not in my book.

Bev: How does Paula deal with her mother?

Art: Oh, she's very clever, from what I hear. Has her own flat just far enough away. Keeps her visits irregular, just occasional visits, mainly to get the computer re-started. Gets her mother talking about herself to avoid fights.

Bev: So there's a bit of a generation gap?

Art: Generation gap? There's a a cultural gap, an intelligence gap, an educational gap, a religious gap, an ethics gap, ...

Bev: Was Paula. born here?

Art: No, came out when she was three. She speaks perfect English, with no accent. Very intelligent, except in maths and physics . . .and football . . . and art..

Bev: So what do you see in her?

Art: Mum, what a question. You are sounding like
       Paula's mother.

Bev: Well, I haven't met her yet, after all these months.
       Are you afraid I might scare her off?

Art: No, Mum. I'm proud of you.

They hug.

Bev: What does she think of your art?

Art: She makes fun of it. We laugh. She mixes up Rodin
       with Rodent. Can't understand how my tiny pieces
       can be so valuable.

Bev: Most women think that size matters

Art: Mum!

Bev: I don't suppose she's into cars.

Art: Not many women are, Mum. You're an exception.

Bev: Oh, I'm only interested to the extent of making a
       sale. I know the buzzwords, but not what they
       mean. Most of the men customers want to do the
       talking anyway, to show off their knowledge, and to
       talk themselves into buying.

Art: How do you deal with these new Cougars?

Bev: Frank handles most of them. I don't mean literally.

Art: I should hope not, but I wouldn't put it beyond him,
       from what I hear.

Bev: He flatters them, shows off his understanding of women, or what he thinks is an understanding of women. He hasn't a clue really.

Art: None of us has a clue. What do we call that gap?

Bev: Emotional intelligence gap?

Art: I don't understand.

Bev: Of course not. Only part of your brain is in your head.

Art: And where's the rest?

Bev: You know very well. I've told you before. . . Are you taking your rattletrap, or do you want my Aston Martin for the night? That might impress her.

Art: Who, Paula? Or her mum?

Bev: Both.

Art: Well, the old girl would think I'm loaded, and start harping about marriage.

Bev: Well, what's wrong with that?

Art: Oh gawd. I can't think of anything worse.

Bev: What, worse than marriage?

Art: No, being harped at. And Paula is a bit of a wild one, under all that black suit lawyer stuff. I think I'll take the bike.

Bev: Ah, you young men just don't understand. Where are the flowers and chocolates? What have you got for her mother?

Art: Good thinking . . . . I'd better pick up a six-pack. You women <u>are</u> a mystery.

Exit Art

Bev: And you men are so predictable!

She shakes her head as she hears off-stage the sound a motor bike, starting revving up and roaring off. Art can vocalise these sound off stage if there are no SFX.

END

AN OFFENSIVE MONOLOGUE

This was first written in April, 2017, and revised in January 2018 and March 2019

It was used in a workshop run by Melting Pot Theatre. The response was woeful – people obviously did not catch on at all. One challenged the veracity of the meeting procedure, one said it lacked emotion, and several revealed that they mixed up the giving and receiving of offence.

Because of this, the monologue was never entered as a ten-minute play, and therefore never presented.

AN OFFENSIVE MONOLOGUE

By Brian Haydon

Cast: A young man or woman.

This is my Third meeting of Offensaholics Anonymous

I am an Offensaholic. I admit that I have this overwhelming desire to be take offense.

Thank you for your applause. It has been very hard to bring myself to stand before you and make this admission.

I realise this affliction is incurable, and learning from our AA brethren, who avoid that first DRINK, I expect we have to train ourselves to not have that first THINK.

I have come to realise that this is a common affliction, and I appreciate the support of this Offensaholics group. We are all in the same boat, except for those of you who can't yet come out and make this admission.

I was impressed by the previous speaker, who was able to report how many days he had achieved offence-free. Ten days without a THINK. That was inspirational. I hope to be able to stand up here and report such progress in future. And of course, there is (local celebrity in audience) who hasn't had a think for years.

Sadly, my addiction to THINKING has a terrible effect on my health, my family and my friends. It has also been a drain on my savings. The stress is eating away at my body. I have high blood pressure, acid reflux and irritated skin, to say nothing of

flatulence, tooth-grinding and the shakes when I get really THUNK.

My partner has threatened to leave me unless I stop THINKING.

I take offence at so many things my children say and do, that I am almost permanently in a state of discombobulation and distress.

I think my friends are avoiding me. Actually, I find that offensive.

He/She tenses up, starts to shake and adopts a growly voice.

After all these years of hanging out together, they have either become addicted to thinking, or they have gone glee-total. (*pause*) Can you imagine, al that amusement and laughter, seeing a sunny side in everything, praising everyone, even politicians!

He/She settles down.

It's a path I must learn to follow. I don't think (oops, slip of the tongue) I don't believe I was born an offensaholic. But there must be some sort of genetic mutation, an inherited propensity. Perhaps it's all nurture, not nature. I do remember my parents becoming catatonic at the mention of the F word. Later I found out there was also a C word that a mere hearing would cause a call for an ambulance.

The other day I saw some people go into a frenzy because the ex-President Obama said the N word. They were shocked,

appalled. Not just one of those tch tch shake your head and put your fingers in your ears episodes. The full frenzy, with bottom sneezes, dropped pens, and calls to their local representative, the council rangers and the media ombudsman. He didn't call anyone a . . . N-word. He just said that there is more to racism than using the word.

I read an article about how children raised in overly sterile environments failed to develop resistance to viruses, and had inadequate immune systems. It is now claimed that the latest university censoring of anyone addressing topics such as racism, religion, mental illness, sexuality and human rights and alternative cultures suppresses the critical reasoning necessary to deal with differing views. In fact, they are creating "safe places" where students are protected from (*shudder*) ideas.

I fell into the temptation. After all, they had the power, and they can be pretty vicious in their ostracism. So I spent my formative intellectual years deprived of debate. In fact, I heard the descriptive words but never heard the other side of issues. It was more important to foster our virtue-signalling, and to make the right gestures of righteousness.

When I entered the workforce, well, not really. When I got a part time job at a call centre, I realised that there are lots of offensive things out there. It's enough to drive you to THINK.

Triggers, they are called. Some are subtle, and we had to be trained in those. But some are just in your face. The worst are the multiple triggers. I saw an elderly lady bump into four cars in the Coles car park the other day. A man called her a "stupid demented old fart" can you believe that? Sexist, ageist,

dissing a disability and using a four-letter word describing bodily function. And "stupid" too. I fainted.

Anyway, I think my upbringing and tertiary education have driven me to THINK. It has made me lose all my friends except old classmates and fellow offensaholics. I've come to this group to find a cure.

Now I understand there are a number of steps I have to take. The first was to admit that I have a problem. Done.

The second was to come out of the closet. Oops. Shouldn't say that. (*Shudder*). The second was to confess to others that I have a thinking problem.

I understand there is aversion therapy available - being turned off thinking by watching commercial TV instead of my safe zone at the ABC. Sure, I can use avoidance strategies. If I withdraw from society I won't be tempted. I can avoid all discussion of anything about which some people disagree. That doesn't leave much to discuss, does it?

There is medication. I can become a zombie, and not read or listen or observe anything. Like the teenagers whose answer to everything is . . . "whatever". Or, the non-committal. "Awesome, man, if you know what I mean . . . Like wow."

He/She transforms gradually into aggression

But let us not be entirely passive in our victimhood. Let us develop our weapons in this grand undertaking, to eliminate offence from our society. Let us develop our vocabulary - recognise the power of words like crass, unacceptable,

disgusting, pompous, pathetic, puerile, stereotypical, callous, platitudinous, hypocritical. Let us know our allies - the human rights commission, the united activists cooperative, victimhood unanimous, Marchers for Every Cause, Society for Letters to the editors, Terrorists of the Twittesphere, Facebook Guerrillas Inc.

Let us be relentless. Let us root out every instance of offence in the community. We have already gained a foothold in community awards- medals and titles in recognition of intolerance.

How dare they refer to our insights as political correctness. It is just correctness, pure and simple. It's compassion, dammit!

Perhaps we are the more intelligent, the more caring, the more productive, the more creative of our species. Stop feeling guilty, friends. Arise, and conquer the world. Shame the offence denialists. Focus on the influencers - the childcare trainers, the one-issue activists, celebrities, the gullible segments of the media. Sensitise them. Shame them. If necessary, bribe, intimidate and expose their pseudo intellectual arguments about free speech.

Beware the great enemy - tolerance. Those who would let offences escape the net, who would turn the other cheek, who would say "sticks and stones may break my bones, but words will never hurt me". What a terrible foe is tolerance. How annoying when a terribly offensive remark (offensive to us ordinary people) just raises a smile, or even worse, laughter. Do not let the comedians and satirists get away with their cruelty, their insensitivity, their callous disregard for the less clever,

He/She pauses, settles down to meekness.

I'm sorry, I reverted there.

But back to my personal problems. I came here tonight to repent and renew. I came to regret and reinvent. But this is not something to be ashamed of.

He/She lapses back into aggression.

Let us <u>not</u> accept that deaf people oops, people with hearing inadequacies, can't be telephone operators, or blind, oops, visually deficient, no, alternatively sighted individuals should be deprived of driving licences. Let us redesign our language to never demean anyone. No more speech defects - just alternative dialects. No more disabilities, just style variations. No more gender, no more status, no more genetic dispositions, no more winners and losers. No more champions, no more competition. Free speech is just protection for the inconsiderate.

Hey, we are nearly there. Our LGBTIQCFU (yes, some people forget camp, fluid and uncommitted) yes, our LGBTIQCFU comrades, our black, oops, aboriginal, oops, indigenous, oops, First Nation, oops, what are they called this year? Anyway, they, and all the support groups for various minority groups and environmentalists have made excellent inroads into stifling debate and changing our language. We defenders of offence have all of their causes at heart.

No, let us harness the spirit of Mao, and eliminate the intellectuals. Let us learn from the inquisition, and demand commitment to the true belief. Let us learn from Lenin, and redefine equality. Let us salute ISIS and the Taliban, for their intolerance of tolerance. Wait a minute. I may have to re-think that. Think about it! Let us celebrate fake news – of the right kind of course.

But wait, that's what brought us here. The evils of THINK.

He/She settles down from her fervour.

Yes, the world is full of temptations.

Drinkers become teetotal. We become thoroughly thoughtless. Tolerant of free speech. Oblivious. Without being inconsiderate, of course.

Our addiction, our affliction, is as bad as the demon drink. I am committed to improving my health, my wealth and, my relationships by ceasing this habit fully and permanently from today. I know you successful reformed thinkers must have some successful techniques. I look forward to learning them.

Thank you for listening.

END

SORRY, DARLING

A Tale of a computer – human interaction.

Presented at Bundanoon Crash Test Drama in 2018. No cigar. Mark Smith played Pat, and Sarah Hawthorn Una.

This is not Sarah!

SORRY DARLING

A Ten-Minute Play by Brian Haydon

Cast:

Pat the Programmer, a geek (either gender)
Una the User, a non-technical person

Two silver boxes, or screens, are on stage, back to audience.
The humans face the audience, but frequently look at and
speak to their mute but voice-recognising computers.
On one side is a geek, Pat the programmer.
On the other is a matronly computer neophyte, Una the
User.
They only speak to the computer, never each other.

Una: You stupid machine. How am I supposed to
        understand "catastrophic error Ref 22B - re-boot"?

Pat: System, I have a new artificial intelligence algorithm
        for you. It makes error messages more human-like.

Una: Catastrophic? Does that mean you're about to burst
        into flames? That may not be a bad idea after all.
        I'm sick of your geek- talk.

Pat: System, close down Error Notifications outine
        Version 23.4, and load "Feminine, Caring, Error
        Notification Sub-System, Version 1.1.

Una: You <u>need</u> a good boot. That might relieve some of
        my frustration.

Pat: You can't find it? System, I taught you to check both
        logical servers and illogical human error
        repositories.

Una: I'll have to call that nice young man form the electrical store.

Pat: No, not suppositories. Are you tuned to Tony Abbot vocabulary setting? Repository! Go check it.

Una: Oh, you are awake! Yes, the one who wiped your entire memory last time.

Oh, wipe that frowning emoji off your face, and get rid of that error message, too.

Pat: No? Try that one the HR department suggested. Personalised Caring version 1.0, code name PC. (*pause*). No? Let me ring the Chief Operating System Technician and see what they finally named the new error program.

Pat picks up phone, dials and waits for answer.

Una: Oh, so you're doing a spontaneous re-boot, are you. Well come back with a friendlier disposition, you useless piece of scrap metal.

Pat: Lois, I just wanted the file name for the error message generator, but now you tell me the whole system has been renamed? Oh, so the marketing folk don't want acronyms anymore? And no i-words, either. I see. No, I don't mean the acronym IC. So what's the error message generator name? "Sorry"? You called the error message sub-system "Sorry"? Wow.

Una: I'll have to pull the plug.

Pat: So what do we call the rest of the system?

Pause

Darling? We call our system "Darling". Wow, how many divorces will that cause? Well, thanks, Lois. No one has updated us.

Una: No, I refuse to save you first. Save me, save me! You aren't worth saving.

Pat: No, don't get upset, Lois, I'm not criticising you. We just weren't told.

Una: System, save yourself, and switch off.

Pat: Oh, don't cry, Lois, I didn't want to upset you.

Una: Don't tell me to stop talking while you shut down, you imbecile.

Pat: It's not your fault. Oops, we aren't allowed to use that word, "fault", are we?

Una picks up her phone, dials.

Pat: Lois, I'll send some flowers for your desk. I'm so sorry.

Una: Jane, can I speak to Ned, please?

Pat: You're only allowed plastic ones? Your boss has a pollen allergy?

Una: Well drag him away from his iPad game, Jane, is that more important than his grandmother?

Pat: I know your office is a no-criticism zone, Lois. That's why I'm sending an appropriate token of my abject failure. I understand.

Una: Yes, he's always about to break the record on Kill the Creeps, or whatever that game is.

Pat: Well how about some chocolates to cheer you up?

Una: Yes, I know I bought him the game for his birthday, but I didn't know it was so violent, and addictive. He just told me what he wanted, and I bought it.

Pat: Sugar-free, organic, fair trade, free-range, chocolates? Sure, I understand. Locally made, fair trade, re-usably packaged, halal . . . oh, don't worry about the halal? OK.

Una: No! Swearing at the computer? Well, I don't blame him for that... oh, he's swearing at the infidels he's about to kill, not at the computer!

Pat: Lois, I have to go. Sorry I upset you. . . Yes, implied criticism is still criticism. Indeed.

Pat hangs up.

Pat: Silly bitch. I'll send her smarties, and see if she takes the hint.

Una: OK Jane, I just wanted some help with my computer. Yes, I know he's only seven, but he knows better than your husband, and the guy at the store, and the NRMA man. I've tried them all.

Pat: So, Darling, uninstall Error Notification V 23, and import File "Sorry" for system "Darling"

Una: Don't worry, Jane, I'm sure our Ned will grow up to be a caring, sensitive man. . . You think that's an oxymoron? Ha. I agree. Bye, love.

Pat: Yes, "Darling"! That's your new name. Don't blame me!

Una hangs up.

Una: Silly bitch! I need a cuppa

Exit Una

Pat: OK, Darling, we're in. Now let's try out your configuration options.

Pat peers at the computer.

First setting "masculine, feminine, neutral or liquid."

I think that should be "flu d", not "liquid". You can't have a liquid gender.

Pause while Pat reads the screen.

OMG! Who's been fiddling with your social circuits? We're not talking about actual gender. We're talking about ways of thinking and communicating.

This isn't a physical matter, like toilets, or qualification for women's sport.

Pause to read again.

I know that's stereotyping. We use the gender convention to give users a choice of conversation types. You know, on the one hand aggressive, assertive, all-knowing – and at the other extreme, docile, submissive, shy.

Pause to read.

You think, oops, put that in quotation marks, that we are implementing a change, soon, to simple, genderless, politically acceptable, non-technical interactions.

We should use modern vernacular for our error messages, you say.

Oh, sure . . . I can see it now. "Yes, No, Like, bummer, dude, you ain't gonna get nuthin' here. You must of, like, stuffed up".

Look, I agree we have to get away from "contact administrator" and "Error 404, page does not exist". But let's not go all fuzzy and . . . I nearly said feminine . . . overly familiar.

No, I'm not getting stressed. But I do think I'll go get a coffee. System, run restart. . . alright, Please darling, run restart.

Enter Una

Una: System, turn on.

No, wait . I read that the CIA can look at you through our computers now. I'd better change first.

Una exits, as *Pat returns* –

Pat: Now, Darling, let's get it on

He looks around to see if anyone is listening, then peers at the screen.

Hmm, they've changed the proposed personalisation settings. There's just one level of obsequiousness, one leve. of sophistication, one level of politeness. Nothing for us techies.

Una returns, wearing an overcoat. preening herself.

Una: Oh, a new message!

Una peers at the screen.

I am politely requested to call you "Darling" in future. You've got to be kidding. Oh, you have new, friendly error messages. That's nice. Sorry? Oh, you don't need to apologise.

Pause to read

And a new app! (*local place*) GOSSIP FOR GRANNIES! Goodie Goodie!

Let's start all over tomorrow.

BOTH IN UNISON   "Goodnight, . . . , darling!"

They both exit (or blackout).

END

THE WEEKEND

This play has never been presented. I thought it would stand out from dialogue-based plays. I have never seen a silent play, but I can imagine this one, quietly satirising the bland 5-day week and the sometimes just-as-bland weekend for young singles.

The couple would wear blank faces throughout, reflecting the ritualised process. I envisage the love-making scene being a tortuously long pose with the girl sitting on the boy's knee, embracing but not moving.

On public transport to and from work, they read and consult phone, and hang onto imaginary strap.

Notes it may be preferable to have 10 minutes of music to get the timing right.

Use of downstage chairs is important.

If desired at crash test drama, extras can be added at the office, pub and club. They interact silently.

THE WEEKEND

By Brian Haydon

Cast: two characters, a male and a female, both early 20s singles.

There is no dialogue.

Where possible and appropriate, they move in unison.

Friday Night

Both of the characters are working at their computers in their offices. He is Stage right, she stage left

At the same moment, they look at their watches, pack up, stand up, check their desks, wave goodbye to colleagues, walk upstage, use elevator.

Each enters separate elevator, towards sides of stage, turn in unison to face audience while riding the elevator.

they walk towards centre stage front. they are now in a pub, she with her friends, he with his. Perhaps interact with front row audience, even comment about the pub's new decor.

They go through the normal pub activities, miming chatting with friends. He plays darts. They occasionally glance at each other.

Then they flirt with each other and exchange telephone numbers.

They exit the pub upstage, turn in opposite directions, travel home by public transport.

They enter their respective apartments simultaneously, watch TV alone, munching snacks.

They fall asleep.

Saturday morning

They wake simultaneously, eat breakfast, wash dishes.

They both vacuum the floor

Saturday afternoon

She works on her hair, her legs, her face.

He pumps iron, checks his muscles in mirror.

Then she performs in front of a m rror, changing clothes, posing, even practising dance moves.

He watches TV, cheering for a football team, then has a shower and grooms himself.

Saturday night

They leave their homes (walk upstage), lock house (in unison).

They arrive at restaurant, sit together, eat, chat silently.

They leave the restaurant, holding hands walking upstage.

They enter club, walking downstage.

They drink , dance, chat, occasionally hug, take turns to tell joke, laugh, show some signs of intoxication.

Leaving the club, he hails a cab.

Sitting in cab cuddling?

They kiss at her door, he makes to leave, but she offers him coffee.

They enter her home (moving downstage)

Beside a chair, they embrace with mounting passion

They make love on the chair (still, silent)

Sunday morning, her apartment.

He gets up and dresses. She is slumped in the chair

He returns home (walks upstage, turns, enters his home)

Back in unison, in their own homes, they act out hangovers - coffee, headache,

Sunday afternoon

They both watch tv, fall asleep.

Monday morning

They wake, shower, dress, make coffee and drink it, look at watches.

They leave their homes by walking upstage, going through door, turning, locking door.

they travel by public transport, enter their offices.

They chat to colleagues, settle at their computers and work. The cycle is complete

END

Jock, Robbie and Rebecca in "What We Want"

WHAT WE WANT

This play was selected by the judge (Michaela Bolzan) as the best play in its heat at Bundanoon in 2018. It featured Jock Bidwell as Roger and Robbie Tabell as Wendy in the heat and the final. Morag Rasmussen played Zola in the heat, and Rebecca Howarth a sassy Zola in the final.

Jock, Morag and Robbie

WHAT WE WANT
A ten-minute play by Brian Haydon

Cast:

Roger,	a professional protester and founder of Whatwewant Inc.
Wendy,	a loyal and experienced employee.
Zola,	Office Assistant.

Scene: *The Company Office. There are two chairs and a table with a computer on it. Roger sits at a desk, speaking on the phone.*

Roger: Thanks for calling What We Want, your Professional Protest Service.

Roger hangs up as Zola enters.

Roger: Hi, Zola, what do we want?

Zola: Skinny people.

Roger: Skinny people?

Zola: Yes, for a protest against sugar tax. They don't want any obese protesters.

Roger: What do we want, sugar. When do we want it? Now.

Zola looks at her watch.

Zola: You want your coffee already?

Roger: No, I'm just doing an outline design for this new project.

Enter Wendy

Wendy: What's going on here?

Roger: Brainstorming. We might have a new project – an anti-sugar-tax protest.

Wendy: Who is the organisation?

Zola: The guy didn't say.

Roger: Probably a front for the fast food industry.

Wendy: Probably. How does that fit with our policy?

Zola sits, pulls up the computer as she says

Zola: I'll look it up. We're over a hundred pages now. We could publish this as the encyclopaedia of political correctness. What would it be under?

Wendy: *(sarcastically)* Try looking up "sugar".

Zola taps and swipes.

Zola: Hmm. Fair trade, Gender diversity in the
                 sugar industry, Indigenous land claims on
                 sugar plantations, "sugar" as a sexist term
                 of endearment – see sweetie, honey.

Wendy: What about obesity?

Zola taps and swipes again.

Zola: Right to be fat, demands for oversized
                 garments. Coca-Cola consumption on our
                 premises.

Roger: What does it say about taxes? What do we
                 want, tax the rich, when do we want it,
                 now.

Zola: Carbon tax, sales tax, GST, . . . nothing on
                 sugar tax.

Wendy: Well we'll need to take a position. Are we
                 for or against a sugar tax?

Roger: Is this likely to be a big account for us in the
                 future?

Wendy: Don't be such a capitalist, Roger.

Roger: Is there a counter movement with a bigger
                 budget?

Wendy: Sometimes I worry about you, Roger.

Roger: Let's accept it then. What do we want. No sugar tax. When do we want it.

All: Never!

Zola: I have to finish cleaning up the stock room.

Exit Zola.

Roger: Wendy, how are we going with this Friday's big demo. Who do we want? Pauline, when do we want her? Now.

Wendy: They expect about 1200 marchers.

Roger: They do like her in Queensland.

Wendy: 300 signs and a big one for the front of the March. "We love Pauline - One nation is all we need - Shed the Burqa".

Roger: We thought of lots more, but our policy is three max, repeated repeatedly. And one slogan - who do we want? Pauline. When do we want her? Now.

Wendy: Don't you think we should be a bit more creative with the slogan, Roger?

Roger: Wendy, you always bring this up. It's recognised worldwide, it's simple, easy to memorise, annoying. What do we want? Simplicity. When do we want it? Now!

Wendy: Back to business. We have four burqa strippers, all quite voluptuous, with flesh covered bikinis underneath. They'll be positioned at the PPPs

Enter Zola, with a big cardboard carton.

Zola: What are PPPs?

Wendy: Primary press positions - where the photographers and cameramen have been told to assemble for the best shots.

Zola points to the cartoon, but Roger ignores her and continues.

Roger: Gimmicks?

Wendy: We're supplying red hair dye, rain resistant, but easily removable with shampoo.

Zola tries to interrupt again – Roger signals her to wait, while asks Wendy . .

Roger: Celebrities?

Wendy: No problem. A couple of Queensland rugby league players. That just cost us a few beers. An Indian Mining Magnate (he paid

<u>us</u>) and blonde Miss Queensland. She was easy.

Zola tries again, but Roger signals to wait – again.

Roger: Arrests?

Wendy: We have three volunteers. Loyal to us, no police records, not very special looking. They have been trained in how to provoke the police - pretty easy in Queensland. They are out-of-work actors. The fake blood clashes with the hair dye, but that can't be helped.

Roger: Good work, Wendy. Now, what did <u>you</u> want, Zola?

Zola: What will I do with these Malcolm Turnbull masks?

Wendy: Burn them!

Zola: What about the toilet rolls with Tony Abbott's face on each sheet?

Wendy: Keep them. He may make a comeback. . . or we can use them ourselves.

Zola: And the condom-shaped balloons from the Barnaby march?

Roger: They were handouts, but no one wanted to be seen blowing them up!

Zola: There's a huge bin of used plastic bags out there. What about them?

Roger: Single use bags?

Zola: Yes.

Roger: Well, put them out in the garbage.

Wendy looks askance, then show disapproval, as Zola exits with her carton.

Wendy: Roger, there are a few problems. The Greens want to disrupt the march. They have been building up their own Protest Services organisation to compete with us.

Roger: How big a threat are they?
Zola: I heard they were having union problems. Their marchers want higher pay, childcare allowances for all protesters, even those with no children, and wet weather penalty rates regardless of the weather.

A moment's silence. They frown at each other.

Enter Zola, waving a phone.

Zola: Battle stations!

Roger: Why?

Zola: Sarah Ferguson.

Roger: What, the royal?

Zola: No. Four Corners have recognised some of
              our protesters. They claim some cases
              where a guy with unique tattoos and a long
              beard has appeared in competing protest
              movements – both for and against a
              Medibank Levy.

Roger: Oh, shite. We have any number of those.
              Zola, look up the emergency procedures
              manual, quick.

Zola opens the tablet.

Roger: What do we want? Mercy! When do we
              want it? Now!

*As Zola reads out the steps, Roger mimes each one (moving
through them quickly)*

Zola: Step one, be unavailable for comment,
              delay, delay.

        Step two, denial, vehemently deny any wrong-doing. Call it
                    Fake News

Step three, old news - claim the guilty party left the organisation some time ago.

Wendy: Yeah, be careful about sacking anyone though.

Zola: Step four, explain the new water-tight procedures. It can never happen again.

Roger: Well, that's fine. And if that doesn't work, turn nasty - discredit the story teller, Sue the ABC for defamation. What else is happening in the market?

Wendy: There's an emerging women's movement wanting power with pathos.

Roger: Great slogan.

Wendy: Yes. They specialise in sad issues, and have group cry-ins with therapy dogs. They also urge men to cry in public, to show they care, and to bridge the gender gap.

Roger: Oh no. It never used to work for Bob Hawke and Kim Hughes, but the ball tamperers got some sympathy. And the macho men can't call them the names they used to, for fear of being called homophobic.

Zola: Power with Pathos is getting lots of donations.

Roger: How's the rest of the market?

Wendy: Oh Roger, always the capitalist. Still lots of
                funding flowing into women's issues. Big
                sympathy for asylum seekers, and rescue
                animals.

Roger: What about Government subsidies? That's
                the only reliable funding.

Zola: And trade unions, of course.

Wendy: The churches and banks have the big
                untapped potential - lots of cash, dictatorial
                organisations, they are coming under
                attack, and they are spending big on
                lawyers, marketing gurus and image
                consultants.

Roger: But they think public protests are beneath
                their dignity. Not for long!

                OK, end of meeting. Let's get stuck into
                Four Corners. Oh, and what about that
                campaign to abolish gender in Victoria.

Wendy: Oh, that's still fluid.

They all freeze. BLACKOUT

END

A Playful Protest

Acknowledgments

I am greatly indebted to Patrick and Gillian Brennan for introducing me to the short play format, and for encouragement along the way. Both have set high standards in their own writing.

Thanks also to local friends for proofreading, suggestions, time-keeping and practice runs & reviewers, in particular the late Ken Challenor and the award-winning playwright and poet Greg Tome.

Much appreciation to the various directors and actors, too many to mention, who have brought the plays to life and revealed subtleties I had not noticed or considered. I am in awe of your art.

Congratulations to the judges who saw merit in the plays, and the audiences who voted for them in competitions or laughed or cried in performances.

Finally, to David McFarlane of Mittagong Print and Design, many thanks for your perseverance and guidance in the art of publication.

David McFarlane

Made in the USA
Columbia, SC
07 December 2021

50613614R00150